Mark,

In the beginning, God . . .

Richard Abbeny

II Timothy 1:7

RANDOM DESIGNER

RANDOM DESIGNER

CREATED FROM CHAOS TO CONNECT WITH THE CREATOR

RICHARD G. COLLING, PH.D.

BROWNING PRESS
BOURBONNAIS, ILLINOIS

Published by Browning Press
3608 N. 2320 W.
Bourbonnais, Il 60914

Publisher's Cataloguing-in-Publication Data
Colling, Richard

> Random designer : created from chaos to connect with the Creator / Richard G. Colling. – Bourbonnais, Ill. : Browning Press, 2004.

> p. ; cm.
> Includes bibliographical references and index.
> ISBN: 0-9753904-0-6
> ISBN-13: 978-0-9753904-0-5
> 1. Religion and science. 2. Evolution–Religious aspects. 3. Creationism. 4. Life–Origin I. Title.

BL263 .C65 2004   2004104358
231.7/652—dc22   0405

Book production and coordination by Jenkins Group, Inc.
www.bookpublishing.com
Interior design by Debbie Sidman/Paw Print Media
Cover design by Kelli Leader

Cover image fractal "The Apple" was created by Philip Northover
http://pnorthov.future.easyspace.com

Author photo by Bill Jurevich – Image Group Photography LLC

Printed in the United States of America
11 10 09 08 07 • 5 4 3 2

Dedication

In loving memory of my sister Debbie,
whose honest spiritual journey began and ended decades
before we understood what she was telling us:
It is always okay to believe the truth.

And there He was all the time,
waiting for His creation to discover Him.

Contents

Acknowledgments

First and foremost, I must thank Sally for her many contributions to this project. For many long walks where we talked at length about God, science, and life; for helping me see that there are many perspectives, each of which deserves respect; and for the endless corrections and retypes of the early drafts. You are a treasure.

Tina Bruner, Rebecca Justice, and Scott Swaim offered invaluable assistance that is greatly appreciated. Ivor Newsham, Larry Watson, and Kent Colling were valued sources of encouragement and support at various stages of the project.

Thanks also to my students, parents Richard and Esther, and each of my four sons, Jeremiah, Landon, Benjamin, and Phillip. These people have unknowingly contributed in so many ways by teaching me about relationships, fatherhood, God, and life. You are my greatest pride and joy. We have learned together. A special thanks also to Jeremiah for developing the *Random Designer* web site.

Preface

Random Designer has been many years in the making, and comes at a time when the forces of science and religion seem to be increasingly at odds with one another. I have watched the debate for decades, believing the flawed assumptions driving this controversy would inevitably be exposed, allowing the truth of science *and* the truth of religious faith to find common ground. Unfortunately, the rhetoric has only intensified and the positions have hardened. The result is an ever-widening chasm within our society that even invades the Christian community. The growing atmosphere of accusation, fear, and distrust is destroying relationships and in subtle ways systematically undermining the credibility of religious faith in general.

I wrote *Random Designer* to help bridge this tragic and unnecessary divide by reassessing some of the most common theological assumptions about God and His creativeness. I recognize the process may be slow: Changed thinking can only take place in minds open to change. Therefore, I hope you will read *Random Designer* as I attempted to write it, with an openness to truth regardless of how it is revealed.

While I believe I have been accurate in the scientific descriptions, I felt that the foundational processes of life must be explained in language that is understandable to non-scientists. Therefore, I ask the indulgence of my scientific colleagues, who will recognize occasional oversimplifications. In a similar manner, I claim no formal expertise in theology. The thoughts in *Random Designer* are my best attempts to reconcile my Christian faith and belief in God with the physical realities of our world.

I do not expect *Random Designer* to be the last word on the subject of science and faith. I suspect that God is continually working, and the profound mysteries of His nature will unfold ever so slowly only as we listen and learn together. It is a journey we all share.

Random Design and Life

Exploring the Foundations of Science and Biology

Random Design—*a powerful method for creating higher order, particularly in living beings. It functions by first generating large arrays of potential building blocks from which the most suitable candidates are sequentially incorporated into an ever-advancing architectural design.*

Life on this beautiful blue planet we call home is a fragile and precious gift. At the same time, it is an enormously resilient thread whose convoluted connections have extended through the dimensions of time and space for eons. The profound mysteries surrounding the nature of life capture our imaginations and intellects as we wonder about our origins and ponder the meaning and purpose of our short sojourn here.

Random Designer is a book about God's creativeness and His desire for relationship with His creation. The first chapter provides a brief review of my personal journey as a scientist and one who holds a strong belief in God. In the second chapter, the creation-evolution issue is met head-on, providing an explanation for the massive misunderstandings that have been promulgated upon our society. The remaining chapters of section I construct an essential scientific foundation for understanding life's most basic principles.

Ironically, randomness is the star of this story! It is the dynamo that commands living things to create order out of disorder in the midst of a sometimes erratic and chaotic world. But there is more to this picture than meets the casual eye, for while randomness is the driver, amazingly, the products possess miraculous elements of design. All of life on earth, including human beings, derives its origin, nurture, and sustenance from this seemingly implausible interplay between randomness and order. Biological processes of development, including mutation, rigid selection mechanisms, large-scale trial and error, and evolution, are just a few of the integral components that contribute to the overall success story. While acknowledging these concepts might provoke some heated discussion, this need not be the case. It is not the aim of *Random Designer* to prove or defend evolution. Evolution is simply taken to be fully compatible with available scientific evidence and also contemporary religious beliefs. The truth is that God made life beautiful, but in no way is it simple.

The culmination of twenty-five years of teaching and research, *Random Designer* offers a truly integrative view of God and our world. During this time, I have developed a greater and more profound appreciation for the mystery and majesty manifested in the miniature molecular architecture and machinery of living cells. No one who has glimpsed this magical world of molecules and cells can doubt that we are indeed fearfully and wonderfully made!

Actually, the scientific basis for random design is not new. The laws of thermodynamics, chemistry and physics that govern the world's physical processes have long been known and understood. What *has* changed is the understanding of how random design plays a pivotal role in determining the very nature of life itself. This new understanding is a relatively recent development. While literally every junior high student today knows that deoxyribonucleic acid (DNA) is the genetic information that guides and controls the development of life, amazingly, this fact was not conclusively demonstrated until 1945. Indeed, modern molecular genetics has an "ancient" history of only about twenty-five years. Knowledge regarding the dynamic nature of the living cell and life in general continues to expand exponentially as scientists achieve understandings of life at levels never before imagined. This new information is fundamentally changing the way life is viewed today, carrying with it great promise, but also potentially disconcerting implications for how our lives should be lived together. Contemporary scientific understanding may even require us to re-evaluate some of our most cherished concepts of God.

Random Designer almost sounds like an oxymoron—a contradiction of terms. Nevertheless, I believe it describes God precisely as He has revealed Himself through His creation. Random design is alive and well in all of biology. Without it, life would not have come into being and certainly could not continue. Not only is random design a foundational component directing the formation and development of life, it also appears to be the best and perhaps the only method that could successfully accomplish the task. Which leads us to the Designer...

Is God a Random Designer—a creator who harnesses the wildness of the universe to accomplish His ends? It seems abundantly clear to me that He is. How we respond to this realization is up to us. We can embrace His methods or we can chafe and resist. Either way, He remains the same. But in many ways, I believe these issues are peripheral. The questions of ultimate import do not center around creation mechanisms, but rather creation *purposes*.

I believe that God has endowed His creation with unbelievable potential, much of which we are just beginning to discover. Meaning, purpose, peace, and fulfillment are fully within the grasp of each individual. In section II, I will expand these thoughts and also share some personal perspectives to help the honest sojourner integrate the processes of random design with a vital and flourishing faith.

It is the ultimate paradox. From randomness and chaos, the Creator has miraculously brought forth His prize and treasure. And now we are granted the mystical opportunity to connect with Him in a personal relationship that touches the very core of our souls!

Beginnings

*In the Beginning, God Created
the Heavens and the Earth*

1

For as long as I can remember, I have wondered about God and His creativeness. As a young child, the Bible stories my parents often read to me relating the power and miracles of God captivated my imagination. I vividly recall a picture of the Garden of Eden. It was a paradise of delicious fruit, brilliant flowers, and lush green plants. Adam and Eve, the caretakers of the Garden, possessed a soft warm radiance that shone from the pages and touched my spirit as an impressionable nine-year-old. The Garden was a magical place: There was no disorder, discomfort, disease, or dying. Everything was perfect.

"Where did Adam and Eve come from?" I asked them.

They related to me that God created the world and all living things in six days, molding Adam from the dust of the earth and Eve from Adam's rib. God was all-powerful and the Biblical story of creation explained how all life began.

This view of creation was adequate for me until high school biology class, where I learned a quite different view—the concept of evolution. I quickly discovered that evolution was a "hot-button" issue for many church people, and they left no doubt as to their strong feelings on the topic. "Evolution is just a weak, unsubstantiated theory," they stated with an assured air. "People who believe in God believe what the Bible says—not that evil evolution teaching."

With this pious pronouncement reverberating in my mind, I attended a private Christian college, majoring in chemistry and biology. It was during my undergraduate college years that I gradually began to see that the stakes regarding this issue were much higher than

I had known. However, I did not recognize the full extent of the tension until I experienced the controversy in a vivid first-hand manner. One evening in the fall of 1976, my wife Sally and I attended a creation-evolution debate at the University of Kansas where I was a graduate student. We arrived on campus that night feeling great curiosity and anticipation. We were especially anxious to hear the ideas supporting creation. After all, we believed in God, and we definitely wanted to come down on the right side of this question! We listened eagerly and attentively to the speakers on both sides, but when the night's discussion ended, I felt dismayed and disillusioned. I definitely had not heard what I had wanted to hear. The so-called creation scientist's arguments had been embarrassingly weak and disappointing. His entire case was based on single-minded attempts to discredit any and all scientific findings confirming evolution, with no regard for the strong merits of the scientific data. Even more revealing, the creationist camp had not engaged in any original peer-reviewed scientific research, nor had they offered any viable scientific alternatives. I confess that I was stunned. But the greater casualty that night was not my faith, but the truth.

Viewing the debate as a non-scientist, Sally saw things quite differently. She was most impressed with the University of Kansas science professor who presented the evolutionary position. Before the debate began, he shared his personal views with the audience, saying that even though he would be representing the position of evolution, he believed in God and his personal faith was vital to him. He also stated he did not see a serious conflict between his religious faith and the scientific discipline he studied and taught.

Several years passed. I finished my Ph.D. in microbiology and immediately commenced postdoctoral studies in tumor immunology. A year later I accepted a university teaching appointment and have served in this capacity for twenty-three years.

During this time, I have continued studying science while teaching university students about the molecular nature of life. At these unseen levels of life, I am awed by the incredible molecular logic that exists within the midst of our cells—an intricate maze of structure, design, and purpose. At times, while explaining some fine detail regarding the human cell, I have faced a lecture hall filled with university biology students and literally felt chills run down my spine as I was gripped by the unbelievable beauty and order so evident in God's living creation.

This understanding has led me to a new appreciation for the striking similarities among all living things, similarities that are often more apparent in the biochemistry and genetics of individual cells than the *outward appearances* of living creatures.

My perspective on the wonder of life continues to grow. Every day the popular press heralds yet another startling scientific development. Causes and cures for cancer are just a few years away; gene therapy has successfully begun in children; agricultural biotechnology is revolutionizing crop yields and improving the environment while promising to feed a hungry world; cloning and stem cell research push us to the limits of science and ethics; and germ warfare, Mad Cow Disease, SARS, and AIDS are everyday concerns. I am thankful that my educational experiences have helped me to understand these scientific developments and their impact on our world. I have been privileged to comprehend the world of God's wonderful creation in ways most of my friends and family may never fully appreciate.

Of course, a complete understanding of life—past, present, and future—remains elusive. There is always more to learn. Nevertheless, in spite of our limitations, each scientific discovery provides new insights into the wonderful tapestry of biological existence. Step by step, scientists are moving closer to a fundamental understanding of life itself. But many questions still remain.

- Will we ever completely understand the mechanisms that make life possible? Will life ever yield its most subtle secrets to science?

- How long will it take? Will it be years, decades, or centuries?

- Is this pursuit even a worthy goal? Are there more important priorities for human scientific endeavors?

- Can our curiosity and desire for learning take us too far? Are moral or ethical liabilities associated with this quest?

Not surprisingly, since so many variables and unknowns are involved, few discerning people take strong positions on these questions. But deeper issues stir even more profound thoughts within us.

- How did the miracle of life begin?
- How did we as humans arrive at our present state?
- Why are we here?
- What is our purpose?

From first-hand experience, I can readily assure you that some outspoken religious individuals and also some especially assertive scientists claim clear-cut authoritative answers to these questions. However, the fact of the matter is that no one completely understands these complex aspects of life. For this reason, it would seem important to exercise tolerance toward each other as we collectively live and learn.

Many people staunchly assert that religious faith and science are incompatible. They live their lives in mortal fear that advances in scientific understanding will somehow undermine their belief in God. This position is perplexing to me, for if we must fear science in order to know God, our concept of Him must be quite small indeed!

A quotation from noted North American psychologist Carl Rogers has been posted on my office door for many years. It reads:

The facts are always friendly.
Face the facts without fear.
Openness reveals your best future.

Of course, one might easily take exception to the idea that facts are always friendly. From personal experience we all know that reality is sometimes downright dreadful. But these words carry an important message: When dealing with uncertainty, the tough questions must be faced honestly and courageously—even if the answers might scare us or threaten traditional ways of thinking.

The truth is that science need not threaten or diminish one's religious faith. Likewise, religious faith need not threaten or diminish science. *And neither science nor faith need be sequestered from reality!*

Today however, in the midst of a heated creation-evolution debate in the public arena and schools, battle lines are clearly drawn at two opposite and equally antagonistic extremes. Personally, I find this development discouraging. Such staunch and rigid positions are neither helpful nor necessary. They alienate people from one another. And most of all, they do not draw anyone closer to God. Therefore, if the most critical objective for us in life is to connect with our Creator (and I believe it is), I seriously wonder if He is pleased with our progress to date. Surely we can do much better.

Many diverse perspectives and rich religious traditions are represented in our world, and each tradition is blessed with a unique frame of reference. In spite of these different heritages, it seems to me that the universal goals of mankind are one and the same—to actively engage in the pursuit of truth and to define a personally satisfying, coherent concept of God. My own concept of God is undoubtedly linked to the fact that I am a scientist. Scientists question, analyze, and attempt to connect things together. In addition, my religious background and experiences as husband, father, and teacher also profoundly influence my thoughts.

This book, then, contains the ideas and perspectives of one broadly trained scientist who is not satisfied with religious platitudes or scientific dogma. I am just like you, attempting to fit the pieces together. *The goal is straightforward—to develop a personal faith and cultivate a close connection with God, while at the same time fully acknowledging the scientific laws and processes that plainly govern our existence.*

Needless to say, integrating science and faith is a daunting challenge, mostly because the target is always moving. As knowledge, understanding, and experience progressively accumulate, the quest becomes an ongoing journey of discovery. No one ever "arrives." In fact, the moment one claims to have arrived is also the precise moment of disqualification from the process.

The truth is that science need not threaten or diminish one's religious faith. Likewise, religious faith need not threaten or diminish science. *And neither science nor faith need be sequestered from reality.*

Over the years, studying science has *strengthened* my faith. I see compelling evidence of God in personal life experiences and also in my academic learning. Every level of biology displays evidence of purpose and design, but these designs are often exquisitely subtle. Therefore, to genuinely see the hand of God at work in creation, we must probe more deeply and embrace *all* truth, regardless of how it is discovered or who discovers it.

Finally, although scientific investigation nearly always contains elements of uncertainty, one clear and important conclusion arises from our current understanding of biology: *Every individual human being is truly unique and special!* Astounding biological individuality and potential are elegantly wrapped up in the very fabric of our being. With this idea firmly in mind, and as we explore the amazing biological details associated with this concept, I believe an even greater appreciation of the Creator lies just ahead.

Above all, I hope this project will convey my deepest personal thoughts about God and life to my four sons, whose relationships I treasure. My heartfelt desire for each of them is that they will come to understand with absolute certainty what their father values most in life. I genuinely hope you will find value as well. I write this book:

- for those committed to an atheistic world-view. Perhaps you will come to understand that there is a reality extending beyond the material world.

- for those who are seeking God and a meaningful relationship with Him, but hesitate to enter this relationship through the doors of established traditional religion. The ideas in this book may offer you a passage key.

- for those already possessing a strong personal faith and belief in God. Perhaps this book will help you touch even deeper levels of experience with your Creator.

Science and Faith

Misconception and Misrepresentation
Lead to Misunderstanding

2

Science is one of the most exciting and satisfying fields of human endeavor because it boldly attempts to interpret and to understand the natural world. The primary goal of science is simple—to learn how things work.

Scientists explore the world using a combination of empirical observation and a systematic evaluation process called the scientific method. Used together, these tools are extraordinarily effective for discovery and learning. Test results, observations, and other findings are integrated together to arrive at reasonable explanations for the world's physical phenomena.

As new insights come to light during an investigation, scientists meticulously assemble this information into the most coherent picture possible. All available resources are used and relevant data is carefully considered to determine how it best fits into an overall understanding of the world.

No doubt, science can be challenging. Multiple and sometimes unknown variables must often be considered at the same time. Therefore, scientific conclusions are initially *tentative*. For example, AIDS was a baffling disease when first observed in the United States in the early 1980s. The fact that the disease affected a wide variety of people among different cultural, geographical, and ethnic groups suggested that an infectious agent might be responsible. But in spite of these early clues, it took microbiologists many months to narrow the number of potential candidates. Early evidence from some quarters suggested that the disease might be caused by a fungus. But after several years of careful testing, scientists had to rethink this notion. The culprit actually turned out to be a previously unknown virus. Today it is known as the Human Immunodeficiency Virus, or HIV. That is how science works—often moving three steps forward, two steps back. And although such an approach may seem somewhat haphazard, it actually has great value because it automatically makes science open to self-correction as new information becomes available.

Science also touches our daily lives and impacts civilizations of the world with a myriad of wonderful creations. Internal combustion engines, computers, cell phones, internet, skyscrapers, heating and cooling systems, nuclear power plants, antibiotics, and life-saving medical treatments routinely extend and improve the quality of our lives. In addition, science teaches us about the fundamental nature of life and the processes that take place within our cells. For example, scientists are hot on the trail to identify each of approximately 30,000 human genes that reside within our 75 trillion body cells.[1,2] These genes contain the coded blueprint of life itself. Knowledge gained from these genetic discoveries and medical science may soon lead to more effective treatments for cancer and other dreaded diseases.

Is our confidence in science well-grounded? We are not hesitant to trust an electrician to wire our house correctly, an auto mechanic to fix our car, an architect to understand the angles of a building project, a chemist to provide the right fuel for our engine, or even a calculator to total our grocery bill. And we certainly trust the scientific understanding of a trained physician when it comes to treating our physical ailments. The applications and technologies that result from scientific inquiry are virtually endless. Science is built into the very fabric of our existence and also our thinking. It has become *the* established and universally accepted method for learning about the physical world—a method that can be understood by everyone. We display faith in science every day, and this trust is uniformly justified because science operates in an atmosphere of openness. New scientific findings are continuously reviewed, evaluated, critiqued, and verified by other science professionals. Therefore, a faulty finding, such as AIDS being caused by a fungus, is generally corrected in short order.

Science at Arm's Length

Most people readily acknowledge science's authority to address questions regarding our physical world, including the origin of life itself. However, some religious groups place one category of science off-limits—evolution. For these people, evolution cannot possibly be true because they understand it to be inconsistent with their religious beliefs. Consequently, the concept of evolution has become a caldron of seething emotions in our society. It has been assigned all kinds of irrational and negative associations—from stealing and murder to comparisons with Adolph Hitler and even Satan himself. And unfortunately, those who understand and appreciate the scientific validity of evolution are often cast in a similar light. But evolution hardly deserves such emotionally charged attention. It is simply a straightforward biological process that explains how diverse life forms, from the simplest to the most sophisticated, are related and how they came into being.

Is it legitimate for zealous representatives of religion to dictate the boundaries of science? Most people would say no. But let me be very clear: This is not an issue that will be legitimately resolved through public opinion polls, popularity, religious beliefs, or politics. Rather, it is a matter of letting science teach us everything it can without being muzzled, even if it leads down paths that might make us uncomfortable. On a more fundamental level, I believe this is a question of whether or not we attempt to limit God.

So why would any reasonable individual attempt to exclude this area of scientific inquiry from discovery and discussion? Although I do not believe there is a rational scientific basis for the exclusionist viewpoint, I believe I understand why some people unfortunately feel they must reject evolution.

Science Versus Value Systems

Consider the following situation. Suppose someone told you about a scientific principle. Provided the information was interesting and not too difficult to comprehend, you would probably listen attentively, hoping to increase your understanding of the world. But what if you had been taught from early childhood that this scientific finding was incompatible with a fundamental religious belief?

Of course, if the information was obviously in error, you would feel no conflict and could reject it outrightly. But even if the information was genuinely true, you might *still* be inclined to reject it because of prior religious convictions. In this way, that which is of greatest importance to you is preserved. This approach (denying reality to preserve a religious teaching) may provide some temporary peace of mind, but it also creates a serious dilemma: Truth is truth and reality refuses to go away!

But what about another possible solution to this dilemma? Suppose the information really *is accurate*, but you find that contrary to what you had been taught, it does not threaten your beliefs. Much to your delight, the new data even confirms and extends your core convictions in ways far beyond your previous understanding. With this new insight you would probably eagerly embrace and incorporate the concept into your core value/belief system. After all, most people readily accept things that validate their personal convictions, especially in the domain of religion.

But hold on—the plot thickens! Just when you have found an acceptable way to integrate your beliefs with the realities of the physical world, you discover to your dismay that a group claiming authority over *all* value systems (we will call them "Preservers of the Faith") lies in wait. Besides objecting to the scientific information themselves, they refuse to let you participate in the community of faith unless you first denounce the science. Now what will you do?

If you are true to yourself, you must reject the authority of the self-proclaimed "Preservers of the Faith." Predictably, they will not be flattered or pleased by your rejection of their mandate, even when it is transparent to all that it was their rigid position on the issue that made the rebuff inevitable. The fact of the matter is that they will find themselves continuously at odds with you and anyone else who believes or provides evidence regarding *anything* that does not support their predetermined views.

This final scenario creates an uncomfortable either/or situation for anyone with a strong sense of personal integrity and strongly held religious beliefs: You must either be true to yourself and leave the community of faith, or deny reality to retain the acceptance of the religious group—a tenuous position to say the least. Not surprisingly, few intelligent people are willing to live within these rigid parameters.

Unfortunately, I believe this scenario describes the current status of the creationist conflict with evolution. A few so-called creationists, who no doubt sincerely believe they represent a strong stand for God, have narrowly defined the terminology and conclusions surrounding evolution. The basic assumption is that science and evolution are incompatible with belief in an intelligent Creator. Therefore, according to the most vocal creationists, we must all reject the "lies" of evolution and science as atheistic, anti-scriptural, and equivalent to evil. Such a declaration may even appear noble in their own eyes—providing protection for their particular religious doctrine. But in addition to being seriously flawed and lacking intellectual credibility, if these responses arise from *intentional* disregard of evidence, they also raise troubling questions of personal integrity, ironically, among those who profess to be the most righteous.

In my view, the explosive conflict surrounding evolution in our culture today is not really about the science at all. It arises from two conflicting worldviews: the atheistic worldview versus a fundamental creationist worldview.

Atheistic scientists are like other atheists. They have made a choice. They simply do not believe there is a God. Their position is based on their academic learning and a variety of life experiences. *If atheists claim that science proves there is no intelligent Creator, it is certainly their right to make that claim. However, it is important to note that their freedom to exercise this right does not make the claim true. Contrary to popular understanding, such a claim is not a logical or legitimate conclusion of science.*

On the other hand, creationists who hold to a very literal story that the earth was created in six twenty-four hour days, fuel the controversy by teaching that evolution is untrue and demeaning to humanity. They are just as adamant as some of the scientists, believing their Biblical explanation provides the ultimate authoritative source. Thus, *all evidence*, scientific or otherwise, must be rejected unless it, a priori, supports their particular interpretation of scripture or a traditional preconceived notion of how God works.

Let me be quick to say that it is certainly acceptable to believe in a literal six-day creation. However, no one can accurately say that science supports this position. Let us be very clear: It doesn't! Few knowledgeable scientists, even those with strong religious convictions, would be comfortable with this claim or would advocate such a position.

Thankfully, some progress has been made in this arena. Indeed, in an attempt to recognize the important role of scientific discovery in our world, the Catholic church and several other mainstream religious denominations have reworded their statements of faith to fully acknowledge the valuable contributions of science, especially relating to our understanding of life and its origins.[3,4]

Some religious conservatives view such church decisions as "caving in" to secularism. These same critical voices proclaim to their loyal troops that evolution is a scientific theory in crisis, and that there is widespread skepticism of its merits and authenticity in scientific circles. It pains me to suggest that my religious brothers are telling falsehoods, but the fact of the matter is that such statements are blatantly untrue. As a thoroughly documented biological concept, evolution has stood the test of time and considerable scrutiny. While scientists routinely debate the *fine details* of evolutionary processes, *they uniformly acknowledge the central features of evolution.* Buoyed by overwhelming evidence from many sub-disciplines of biology, evolution has become *the* working model. No serious scientific alternatives have surfaced—none! Evolution is the only current and viable scientific framework that provides a rational understanding of the immense and beautiful diversity of life on our planet.

Evolution and Public Education

The teaching of evolution in the public schools has become a hotbed of explosive controversy. This development is both tragic and unnecessary. While apparently not so obvious to the combatants, the root of the problem is really quite simple: The basic underlying assumption is flawed. Both atheistic scientists and also fundamental religious folk *mistakenly* believe that if evolution is real, this means that there is no God. I am pleased to provide some clarity to this issue! This assumption is flat wrong! To be sure, I am fully aware that many people hold strong sentiments on this issue. However, I must also add that unfortunately, emotion and religious fervor invariably seem to trump reason. I say these things from the depths of my heart hoping that people will take them in the way they are intended. Nevertheless, in both scientific and religious circles misunderstanding continues to abound.

The truth is that evolution is an integral component of biology. It should be included as an essential part of a comprehensive science educational effort. The problem arises when the interpretation and meanings of evolution are extended too far. For example, if evolutionary scientists go so far as to require an *atheistic* attachment to the teaching of science in our public schools or to scientific inquiry relating to life's origins, a predictable, fierce, and legitimate protest would and *should* ensue. Such a position goes far beyond defensible scientific observation or interpretation. To gain a proper perspective on the subject, we must understand that *teaching scientific evolution in schools is quite different than teaching atheistic evolution.* Unfortunately, the current highly publicized debate in education today regarding the teaching of evolution continually seems to miss these subtle, but critical distinctions.

Science, Evolution, and Religious Belief

Evolution can be viewed in one of two ways. First, evolution is a self-governing and self-propagating process arising from God-less natural laws (God does not exist), or secondly, a Master Designer devised the natural laws of life and uses evolution to accomplish His purposes (God does exist).

Interestingly, an atheistic scientist might review the scientific literature and decide there is no God, while another scientist, given the same information, might reach a totally opposite conclusion—there must be a God, an incredible Master Designer who is far beyond us. Same science, but totally opposite conclusions.

How can this be? To answer this question, it is important to recognize a critical truth about the nature of these two conclusions—a fundamental fact that lies at the very core of the creation-evolution controversy. *Science cannot prove or disprove either conclusion!*

Atheists can never probe deeply enough into the natural laws of our world to exclude Him, and while scientific theists see strong evidence for creative design, they find that science cannot always legitimately address questions regarding the who and why of things. Ironically, at the precise moment we scientifically proved or disproved God's existence, our definition of God would have to be changed.

> If atheists claim that science proves there is no intelligent Creator, it is certainly their right to make that claim. However, exercising this right does not make the claim true! Contrary to popular understanding, such a claim is not a logical or legitimate conclusion of science. To gain a proper perspective on the subject, we must understand and acknowledge that teaching *scientific* evolution in schools is quite different than teaching *atheistic* evolution in schools. This distinction may appear to be rather subtle, but it is a crucial point to consider if we ever hope to bring peace to the controversy.

Most proponents of the two extreme viewpoints of God-less atheism and science-less creationism refuse to consider a more accommodative third option. This *third* position fully supports scientific inquiry, yet also affirms the existence of a Master Designer. It implies that faith and science are not mutually exclusive, as both atheists and creationists presently seem to insist. Many variations of this thought exist, but most people would categorize it as a type of theistic (God-initiated) evolution.

Is there hope for reconciliation? Can our faith coexist and flourish along with scientific advancement? I genuinely hope so. However, it seems clear to me that progress will only take place as we allow science and faith to freely speak in the areas over which they have authority.

Larger Issues

Science reveals a great deal of evidence for design and for the concept of an implied designer. But scientific studies primarily address mechanisms—the how of things. In doing so, they provide us with wonderful insights into how the world and living things are assembled. However, science *does not* offer definitive answers to other questions.

- Why was I created?
- What is the purpose of my life?
- How shall I regard others and God?

People who hold science to be the final authority sometimes fail to recognize that the scientific approach has built-in limitations. Science can teach us about weather systems, electricity, and how cells communicate with one another, but it cannot show love and compassion.

Please do not get me wrong. Scientific inquiry holds great promise for our society. We should not diminish the authority of science in areas where science is qualified to speak. What I am saying is that science has little to say about many of the most vital aspects of our existence—things such as values, relationships, and the purpose and meaning of life.

Some scientists look for meaning *through the process of science.* In a society where values, like fashions, seem to change with the seasons, we are often led to believe facts can be determined by public opinion polls or celebrities who espouse a certain viewpoint. Therefore, it is good to have a group of people who adhere to a logical process; individuals who believe that facts *can* be established and are distinct from, and not subject to, mere opinion. In this sense, science is useful and rewarding.

In addition, it is gratifying to discover things about the world we live in. Solving a tough problem, curing a disease, or increasing our understanding of the world and ourselves creates immense personal satisfaction. Science really can be fulfilling and even fun. But in and of themselves, these accomplishments lack greater significance.

So many things we do each day seem important. But when reality rudely intrudes in the form of a lost job, a broken relationship, serious illness, or the death of a loved one, we realize what is truly meaningful in life. Only then do we pause from our frenetic pace and realize our busyness and the process of accumulating more things can not satisfy our deepest and most heartfelt needs.

The message is consistent: Science is no substitute for quality relationships. It is our faith in a reality beyond the physical dimension that leads to the ultimate meaning and purpose for which we were created.

I believe the creation-evolution debate is fruitless and even harmful to humanity. It arises from a hopeless insistence by some that science can prove the *why* of our existence, and an arrogant, ill-informed insistence by others that faith can explain the *how*. Neither of these positions is reasonable nor defensible. *It is time for science and faith to embrace and find common ground.*

Undoubtedly, some individuals from both science and religion will reel at such a repugnant idea. However, significant progress will only be made when science and religious faith search *together* for what is important in life. As a tool, science can enhance our faith and help us understand life's purpose and meaning. Likewise, religious faith can help us approach science with a much-needed and more sensitive human touch, as together, we address the truly tough problems of our world.

And somehow, it seems to me the Master Designer intended it to be that way from the beginning.

The Driver

*A Paradox Powers and
Sustains All of Life*

3

Anything left to itself tends to deteriorate and fall apart, becoming disorganized and less useful than it was before.

Suppose you spend an afternoon and build a beautifully sculpted sand castle on the seashore. The elegant pointed towers and smoothly shaped walls draw admiring glances from everyone passing by. But if you leave for the night and return to the beach the next day, you will discover to your dismay that the towers have tumbled into the surrounding canals, and the walls have crumbled into dry, grainy heaps of sand.

In the same way, a neglected house gradually falls into disrepair, and a car that is never washed corrodes and disintegrates. Even our physical bodies require regular maintenance. Without proper care these marvelous creations suffer premature death and decay, returning to the simple nonliving organic chemicals, from whence they came.

This destabilizing trend is easy to see in many aspects of our everyday lives. But what is this mysterious law that dictates decay, death, and destruction?

The Second Law

Scientists describe this tendency toward decay as the Second Law of Thermodynamics. It is one of three fundamental laws of nature governing all structure, form, and chemical reactions within the physical universe. No one seems to know where the Second Law came from or how and why it came into being. But careful scientific evaluation and observation clearly demonstrate the reality of its existence. It is a consistent predictable law that helps us understand how the physical world changes.

In its primary role, the Second Law of Thermodynamics dictates the directional flow for all physical and chemical reactions. The direction of this flow is always from high structure to low structure. Sand castles deteriorate, cars fall apart in the junkyard, and our bodies wear out with age and die. Put simply, all structure tends to become more unstructured. In a larger sense, the whole of the physical world exists as a continuum, or scale, of random states. At one end of this continuum complete randomness prevails, while the other end is highly organized. Visualize a heap of dry sand versus a sand castle.

Properties of the Second Law apply to both matter and energy—components that we associate with the real physical world. So, in this sense, matter and energy are related. Albert Einstein, the noted physicist, recognized and described this relationship in his revolutionary equation of relativity: $E=mc^2$.[1] Consistent with this expression, when matter breaks down into simpler components, the de-structuring event is typically accompanied by the release of large quantities of energy.

The Second Law of Thermodynamics is vital to the concept of random design. It acts on a variety of levels, many of which are readily apparent, as in the sand castle analogy. But thermodynamics also influences reactions at the invisible and most elemental levels of chemistry, physics, and biology. For example, place a few drops of blue food coloring into a glass of water and watch what happens. Within seconds, the colored molecules move from high concentration to low concentration as they uniformly disperse throughout the solution. The event is both fast and spontaneous, requiring no overt external force to proceed. The process is also basically unidirectional, or one-way. Except in a reverse video sequence or by utilizing some external assembling force, we would never expect the blue food coloring to spontaneously re-concentrate. In a similar manner, if you touch a red-hot stove, the concentrated heat quickly randomizes from the burner to your finger—a painful lesson in the Second Law of Thermodynamics.

Therefore, provided a suitable conducting medium is present, the Second Law commands that things will always move from a more structured state, or higher concentration, to a less structured, or more randomized, lower concentration. This idea is illustrated in Figure 3.1.

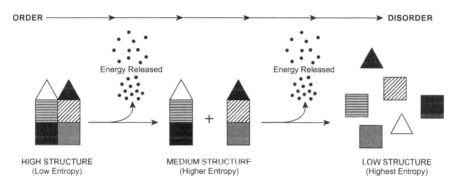

Figure 3.1   Directional Tendency of Second Law Is Toward Maximum Disorder

The Second Law is the governor of all physical phenomena, and when it is fully satisfied, the final fate of the universe will be total random energy and disorder. Physical scientists sometimes describe this universal chaotic state as "entropic doom." But there is no cause for alarm. This scenario is many billions of years in the future.

The Second Law can be defined with an equation called the free energy equation. Before publishing his provocative book, *A Brief History of Time*, Stephen Hawking was warned that every equation included in a book cuts the book sales in half.[2] He could not contain himself and included one equation. I will also limit myself to just one. But because some may find the Second Law to be a bit technical, I will describe it as well as represent it mathematically. This Second Law is vitally important because it establishes an essential foundation for random design. The free energy equation, which defines the Second Law in mathematical terms, is given here.

$$\Delta G = \Delta H - T \Delta S$$

The free energy term (G) represents the theoretical maximum amount of energy that can be derived from any reaction. As we will see shortly, this free energy is critically important because when it is released it can subsequently be used for constructive purposes. Heat energy is represented by the symbol H; S is the entropy, or randomness, term; and T represents the value for temperature. The delta (Δ) symbol is a scientific descriptor that simply denotes a numeric change (either positive or negative). Now let us examine how these components interact with one another to produce an unexpected and truly remarkable phenomenon.

The most important variables in this equation are the heat (H) and entropy (S) terms. Temperature is of lesser significance because biological organisms, especially those that are warm-blooded, do not experience large changes in body temperature.

Utilizing this mathematical relationship, scientists can calculate free energy values (G) for any physical event.* The ability to accurately measure the change in free energy (G) is important because it lets scientists gauge the likelihood that a reaction will actually occur. Some things change readily, while others do not. Reactions that would release large amounts of free energy are the most likely to proceed (be spontaneous), and the more free energy released, the more spontaneous the reaction will be. Take the burning of gasoline for example. Combustion of liquid gasoline (structured) into its less structured gaseous products of carbon dioxide and water vapor not only releases huge quantities of heat energy (H), but the process also dramatically increases the overall entropy (S) or randomness, of the system. Acting together, the released heat and entropy are powerful forces, generating huge increases in free energy (G), and thus compelling

---

* Those who examine this relationship carefully may note a discrepancy between the textual description and the mathematics. For example, according to the equation, if entropy increases, it would appear to cause a decrease in free energy, not an increase. The reason for this apparent discrepancy is that increases in free energy (G) and heat energy (H) are associated with negative numbers. In other words, the more negative the number the greater the energy.

the reaction to progress to completion. I recognize that it would be very easy for a casual reader to miss the full significance of this principle, but please take note because the practical consequences of these subtle phenomena are absolutely stunning.

Without the Second Law and its inherent quality to make physical matter and energy randomize, nothing in the world would happen. Everything would stop. There would be no chemical reactions, no physics, no connections, no movement, no life—nothing! In a very real sense then, the Second Law is an incredible, unseen, universal driver. It energizes everything in our world and in the universe—to move!

The Second Law and Time

Hopefully, it should be clear by now that organized structure tends to randomize into simpler components, releasing energy in the process. This understanding then leads to another question—how fast?

Interestingly, the Second Law does not specify how quickly a structured substance will convert to a more random product. In fact, time appears to be a total non-issue. The Second Law only dictates ultimate outcomes. Consequently, even though a reaction could take place immediately, this does not mean it will. The change could occur right away or it could take a long time—perhaps years, or even millions of years.

This part of the Second Law is obviously good. Consider what would happen to our world if the Second Law demanded the immediate obedience of every structured entity in existence. A sudden, violent rush to randomness would ensue throughout the whole universe. All possible reactions would instantaneously proceed amid a veritable explosion of chaotic energy, until there was absolutely nothing left to randomize. Such an event would produce the entropic doom scenario mentioned earlier in the chapter, except in this case, it would happen in one huge blast instead of occurring over billions of years. This devastating, explosive inferno would leave absolutely nothing behind—no structure, no reactions, no life, nothing but the eerie buzz of total and complete randomness.

Fortunately, all structure does not break down at once, which suggests that built-in constraints are imposed upon the Second Law. Indeed, limitations are present, but they are only temporary. Sooner or later, everything moves toward the state of ultimate randomness, but some forms of matter move faster than others. In short, the universe is like a timed-release capsule.

> . . . The Second Law is an incredible, unseen, universal driver. It energizes everything in our world and in the universe—to move!

Incentives Are Required for Physical Reactions to Proceed

Whether fast or slow, even the most spontaneous reactions (changes) need the right conditions before they will proceed. Consequently, virtually every physical reaction requires energy as an incentive. Elevated temperature, increased concentration, or even a physical push can neatly do the job. For example, a match flares quickly when it is struck against a rough surface that provides frictional heat. Water at high levels in a reservoir rushes through power turbines when a passage is provided. And a rock poised atop a cliff crashes to the bottom if it is pushed.

The critical amount of energy required to start a reaction is called the *energy of activation*. Every physical and chemical reaction has its own special requirements for the type of energy and the amount needed to move it to a product. Reactions needing only a small energy input proceed easily and quickly. Reactions calling for stronger incentives occur much more slowly. Nevertheless, whenever the critical activation energy requirements are achieved, the reaction promptly progresses to the most stable corresponding product.

Popping corn illustrates this concept nicely. If you combine fresh popcorn kernels with vegetable oil in a pan, nothing significant happens. You would wait a very long time for the corn to pop on its own. In fact, it probably never would. However, if you apply energy in the form of heat to the oil and seeds, the spontaneous popping reaction begins the moment the seeds absorb a critical quantity of the heat. The amount of heat needed by the popcorn seeds before they transform into fluffy white product is the energy of activation. Once the seeds have overcome this energy barrier, the reaction proceeds to its delicious conclusion. As predicted by the Second Law, large quantities of heat are also released, and the end product is more disordered and less compact than the original popcorn kernels. In most cases once a spontaneous reaction of this magnitude takes place, the product is so radically different, it can never return to its original state.

In summary, the world around us encompasses an infinite number of potential spontaneous reactions. But each reaction actually takes place only when conditions are just right.

A Paradox—Constructive Synthesis Reactions

So far I have portrayed the physical world as proceeding headlong toward chaos, disorder and destruction, a direct commandment of the Second Law of Thermodynamics. There is, however, a problem with this picture: Reactions are not always destructive. No one can deny that complex design and structure are evident all about us, especially in the domain of life. Bacteria, insects, plants, animals, and humans are all vivid examples—highly ordered life forms that have been created from less organized molecules and cells. Obviously, mechanisms capable of producing order from disorder must be functioning here, or life could not exist.

At first glance, synthesis reactions—those creating structured products—seem to be at odds with the destructive demands of the Second Law of Thermodynamics. But if this is true and constructive synthesis reactions must move in a direction forbidden by the destructive tendencies of the Second Law of Thermodynamics, how is *any* structure or synthesis feasible?

Fortunately, scientists know the answer: *Constructive synthesis reactions can and do take place, but only when a significant outside energy source is provided. They do not occur on their own.*

Sand castles do not build themselves. They require energy input, in this case from a person. Cars do not move without fuel. They need the energy released from the combustion of gasoline. And living organisms cannot grow new cells and tissues without a continuous source of food energy.

Coupled Reactions Are Creative

To review our thoughts so far, spontaneous decomposition reactions *release* energy, while synthetic reactions *require* energy. Biologists have learned that when spontaneous reactions generate free energy, some of this energy can be captured and used to create novel structure. Because these combined reactions physically connect spontaneous breakdown reactions with constructive reactions, they are called *coupled reactions.*

For example, when we eat a meal the chemical energy stored in food is released within our bodies during the breakdown process of digestion. Some of this energy is captured to make strong bones, muscles, and other tissues. This process relies on one overriding requirement: Total energy released from the breakdown of food must exceed the energy required to support the body. A healthy body supplied with a proper diet of food easily fulfills this requirement, and the Second Law of Thermodynamics is thus fully satisfied. Figure 3.2 illustrates this concept.

Coupled chemical reactions are critical to our discussion because they are the essential link between chaos and order. In this way, random, spontaneous breakdown reactions actually serve a *useful* purpose, forming the essential cornerstone for the establishment and continuation of life on our planet. They provide the energy, resources, and the drive that make life possible.

The Main Molecule of Life—Glucose

Living organisms use diverse energy sources for coupled synthetic reactions, but of all these molecules the sugar glucose is

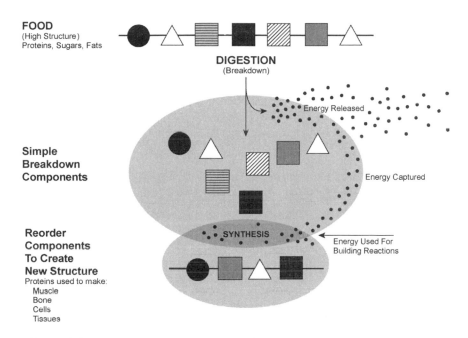

Figure 3.2 Coupled Reactions Are Creative

most important. Without glucose, most, if not all life on our planet would likely come to an abrupt end. Therefore, an inexhaustible source of this common sugar must be provided.

Fortunately, the mechanisms for generating massive quantities of glucose have been operating on earth for billions of years. The sun's radiant energy, captured through photosynthesis, converts carbon dioxide and water into glucose and other related "high structure" substances. Virtually all living things, from the smallest simple bacteria to complex human beings, use glucose as the universal fuel for biological construction. Indeed, some bacteria can produce every component of their cell structure from glucose alone. Thus we see the essential role of sunlight: Either directly or indirectly, it fuels the formation of all higher life. Plants capture the energy, animals eat the plants, and we eat the plants and animals. This type of biological connection is called a biological food or energy chain.

Living organisms perform these matter-energy conversions with incredible efficiency. Under optimal conditions, cells are able to capture nearly 40% of the energy available in glucose. This number is even more impressive when compared to mechanical energy conversions that are typically much lower. Thus, biological systems not only perform amazing feats of energy capture and inter-conversions, they do so with incredible economy.

Finally, certain logical consequences arise from the matter-energy conversions discussed in this chapter. Perhaps the most significant one is the fact that life itself can be created and maintained on our planet by tapping into the sun's energy supply. But the incredible achievement of creating and sustaining life is only temporary. All living things ultimately die and decompose. During the process of decomposition, life's assembled components once again break down into the simple molecules from whence they came, ceding back to nature their accumulated structure and energy. In this sense, all of life and biological structure are cyclic and fleeting. Ashes to ashes—dust to dust.

It seems like a mysterious paradox. Emanating from the raw forces of unbridled chaos and randomness, unanticipated creative powers and pathways have emerged. As human beings, we share a common physical challenge with every living creature on our planet. That challenge is to endure.

There can be no doubt that our efforts to harness these powers of randomness to build and synthesize—to develop, press forward, and simply survive, are continuous, difficult, never-ending, and uphill struggles. The Second Law tugs and pulls at *all* structure, seeking to bring life to its ultimate destiny of death and destruction. And as sobering as it seems, from a *strictly physical perspective*, in the final analysis the Second Law always wins.

But the Random Designer is not concerned: He sees a bigger picture. The Second Law is simply a necessary part of His magnificent plan.

Upon This Foundation

The Universe Is Born

4

The previous chapter introduced and discussed the Second Law of Thermodynamics, showing how it serves as a driver by propelling reactions forward to their logical completion. The whole of creation depends upon this law to funnel energy into productive pathways. The most magnificent synthesis of all is that unusual and improbable creation we call life.

How do spontaneous, randomness-driven reactions produce such an amazing result? To answer this question, we must start at the beginning.

The Universe, Stars, and Chemical Elements

The story of life begins with the formation of the universe. According to current scientific views, the universe came into being approximately 13 to14 billion years ago.[1] At that time, all observable matter was concentrated into an ultra-dense region of space, and this accumulation resulted in a cataclysmic explosion. Scientists call this explosion the Big Bang.

The Big Bang produced incredibly high temperatures, and as the force of the blast radiated energy outward, the new dimensions of time and space came into being. The universe was born. Initially, the explosive inferno produced such extreme heat and kinetic energy (energy of motion) that no discernable structure was present: The early universe was formless and void. However, scientists believe that within a few hours gradual cooling took place and nearly all existing matter assumed the form of two chemical elements—hydrogen and helium.

Eventually, as the newly formed matter cooled, gravitational attractions caused the hydrogen and helium to condense together, leading to the formation of early stars as nuclear fusion reactions, similar to those of our sun, were fired into existence. Amidst these fusion reactions, the concentrated hydrogen and helium systematically experienced a chain of spontaneous nuclear transformations, giving birth to the entire family of diverse chemical elements observed in our world today. These were among the first random reactions to create stable organized form.

I am sure you can all recall the periodic table of elements from your high school science or chemistry class, right? This table is significant because it allows us to view the composition of the whole physical world on just one chart. Each element on the periodic table contains unique combinations of protons, neutrons, and electrons that impart to the element its physical characteristics. The observed occurrence and frequency of the elements in our world today are a reflection of their overall rates of formation as well as their innate stability. The stars then, are the original birthplace of all the chemical elements and of our own physical reality. As children of the stars, the 112 known chemical elements provide the foundation for our bodies and the rest of the physical world.

Although the early physical transformations of the elements are certainly remarkable, chemical elements are not alive. Therefore, if we are to gain an understanding of life, we must understand which combinations of elements enabled life to appear on our dead planet. When discussing the chemistry of life, one chemical element stands above all others. It is the element carbon.

Life-Giving Carbon

Carbon is indeed a very special element, providing the basic chemical backbone for all living organisms. But why was carbon selected over all other elements to serve as the foundation for life?

Biochemists (scientists who study the chemistry of life) know that carbon is particularly well suited for its important life-giving role. For example, it has the ability to form stable chemical bonds (connections) with its parent element hydrogen, resulting in a molecule called methane. In addition, various combinations of carbon and hydrogen give rise to infinite numbers of larger molecules. These substances, called hydrocarbons, play many key roles in living systems. They are the molecules that form the membranes of living cells and also serve as a foundational basis for simple compounds, such as vegetable oil, fats, gasoline, and plastics.

The innate ability of carbon to bond (connect) with hydrogen and several other elements is vitally important. Such interactions produce complex molecules with very distinctive and special properties. For example, hydrocarbons carry no electrical charge, and since water has a charged character, uncharged hydrocarbon molecules tend to segregate themselves from a water environment. We can easily view the effects of this sequestering property when a drop of vegetable oil floats on water, or when an oil spill from an ocean tanker drifts ashore. As we will see later, this simple molecular preference to not mix with water is one feature that makes biological structure possible within the context of an aqueous or water environment.

Besides forming hydrocarbons, carbon also establishes stable chemical connections with other elements, such as oxygen, nitrogen, sulfur, and phosphorus. And although each element has its own binding characteristics, electrical charges, and other physical and chemical properties, the ability to combine with carbon produces a new level of synthesis and structure. These carbon-containing compounds are the basis for organic (carbon-based) chemistry. And with organic chemistry comes the potential for synthesizing the core molecules of life. But this capability also leads to some legitimate questions. How did the first organic molecules form on our primitive planet? What were the conditions, and how long did it take? These are difficult questions. To begin to understand, we must acquire a sense of the enormous time frames involved.

Early Earth and Time Frames

Geologists believe that earth came into existence approximately 4.5 to 5 billion years ago, formed by collapsing dust and debris—remnants of the Big Bang. Of course, everyone would agree that 4.5

billion years is certainly a long time and difficult to fully comprehend. However, to help us develop a perspective of possible events, it is important to understand the enormity of such a time frame.

Consider that one billion minutes ago, the year was approximately A.D. 102, and the early Christian movement was just being organized. Four and one-half billion minutes ago the date was approximately 6560 B.C., several thousand years before the Sumerians of ancient Mesopotamia established the first recorded history of humanity with written pictograms. As a more relevant reference, if the earth's entire history of 4.5 billion years was condensed into one calendar year, the last 2,000 years would take place in the final sixteen seconds of December 31st, and a typical life span of eighty years, extending backward from the present, would take place in the final six-tenths of a second of the year. Clearly, these short periods would hardly be enough time to grasp a realistic view of what happened during the whole preceding year. In a similar manner, it is very challenging for scientists to trace the early history of earth and the life that has appeared. A billion years is a long, long time.

These facts present a significant stumbling block to our minds: Our limited frame of reference stifles our overall perspective. It takes a strong sense of imagination to conceive how incredibly old our planet really is and how remarkably creative it has been over this vast time period.

Requirements for Life

Although the planet's birth was wild and turbulent, the birth stage was only one chapter for earth. During the next phase, the proper environment and essential raw materials necessary to sustain life were generated. But what were the special ingredients needed for this neonatal planet to itself give birth to life?

Time was the first requirement, the second was an accumulation of specialized molecules with the potential to assemble into living form, and finally, earth needed one or more reliable energy sources.

Adequate Time

According to the best scientific evidence, approximately one billion years elapsed before the first primitive life appeared on the planet. This extended period before life's appearance (prebiotic) was not a trivial matter. In fact, it may have been crucial. Indeed, nearly one-quarter of the earth's history or 1.2 billion years, was apparently spent simply preparing the planet for its destiny of creating life. Given the immensity of the planet and the obstacles to synthesis inherent in the Second Law, it seems surprising the process was ever successful. One might even call it a miracle.

Specialized Molecules

While no one knows the precise composition of the early earth's atmosphere, scientists who have investigated possible environments during the earliest time in earth's history have some ideas as to which simple molecules may have been present. Mostly gases arising from the upper mantle of the cooling earth, these candidate molecules included, among others: nitrogen, hydrogen, ammonia, hydrogen cyanide, methane, carbon dioxide, formaldehyde, and water.[2,3] Precisely which substances actually gave birth to simple biochemical structures and how they did so is a more difficult question, which will be addressed shortly in more detail.

Energy Source

Finally, the need for an energy source was critical. Based on the principles of the Second Law discussed in the previous chapter, it is easy to understand that suitable energy sources are needed to fuel the formation of even the simplest living molecules. Remember that organized structures do not form by themselves.

In its relatively newborn state, the earth probably contained several usable energy sources. Sunlight, particularly ultraviolet (UV) radiation; heat from the cooling earth's core; and radiation from the continued nuclear transformations of the elements were all viable candidates. In addition, strong electrical storms and some non-carbon inorganic compounds may also have played a role.

Marvelous Molecules of Life

The key question scientists ask is how our prebiotic (pre-life) planet, given sufficient time, energy, and resources, created and accumulated building blocks for the first life form. To begin this discussion, we will identify the types of molecules that were needed.

The simplest way to determine which ingredients are most essential for life, is to observe the chemistry of contemporary living organisms. By doing this we see that from the most ancient bacteria to highly developed human beings, certain molecules are common to all living forms. Sugars, amino acids, and fatty acids are examples of such molecules with central roles in the most basic processes of all living cells. Taken together, these observations suggest that these common molecules were present in the most primitive life forms and have continued to carry out essential life-giving roles over billions of years.

The question to be addressed is a simple one: Is it possible to create these and other simple biological molecules from the resources available on the early earth? To gain insight into this question, scientists simulate prebiotic conditions and observe whether or not specialized organic molecules are able to be formed. But before we proceed with this idea, there is an important caveat to keep in mind. Demonstrating that all the essential molecules *can* form under simulated prebiotic conditions does not prove *how* they actually formed, or even that they formed at all. No one can go back in time to conduct the "real" experiment. Nevertheless, the ability to synthesize such molecules seems to be an absolute prerequisite for life's beginnings. And if biochemical synthesis events can be observed in a laboratory today, then the basic concept of prebiotic synthesis would also seem reasonable.

In 1953 a noted American scientist named Stanley Miller initiated this line of investigation, conducting an experiment that simulated environmental conditions he believed to exist during prebiotic times.[4] For his simulation, Miller basically used a heated flask of water, salts, and gases like ammonia, carbon dioxide, hydrogen, and nitrogen. He provided two energy sources—heat and an electrical discharge to simulate lightning. This experiment was allowed to continue for a period of two weeks and the results were spectacular. Refluxing or mixing the gases with the energy sources produced many diverse biological molecules. Included in the mix were a variety of amino acids at concentrations approaching 10^{16} (10,000 trillion) molecules per milliliter. (A milliliter has a volume about the size of a pencil eraser.) Other simple organic compounds also formed in these studies, and these results have been confirmed and extended by other scientists who have conducted similar simulation experiments, but under a variety of different conditions. No doubt these experiments have had a significant impact on scientific thinking, but the results are often over-extended or misconstrued.

An important thing to note about Millers' experiment is that it does not presume to have solved all questions regarding prebiotic synthesis reactions. In fact, most scientists today believe that real atmospheric conditions of early earth were quite different than Miller's simulation. The most important conclusion to be drawn from these experiments is that they simply demonstrate the plausibility of prebiotic synthesis producing life-giving organic compounds.

Meteorites are another source of organic molecules. Astronomers and geologists know that massive meteorite storms bombarded earth during the first billion years, and many scientists believe these storms contributed vital elements to the organic pool of building block precursors. Interestingly, many organic molecules found in meteorites are the same as those observed in Millers' experiments and are present in similar ratios.[5] Once again, such studies do not prove that prebiotic syntheses occurred in this way, but the accumulated results show that the simple raw materials of early earth could be remarkably productive.

It seems that a lifeless planet, created from a massive explosion and condensation of random gases, once faced the task and opportunity to fulfill its destiny. Part of that destiny meant using available resources to create simple precursor molecules that might someday initiate life itself.

Was earth up to the task? The available evidence suggests that it was more than capable. Although scientists do not understand all the details, we must seriously entertain the possibility that synthesis reactions may have actually occurred even more readily than originally believed. This knowledge suggests that the earth and her elements were, in fact, pregnant with life from their inception and by their created nature. Adequate precursor molecules, water, and energy sources were all present. The only thing required for them to initiate their life-giving magic was that these precursors be organized into more complex assemblies.

Random Creation—
Divine Selection

Life's Molecules Arrive on the Scene

5

In chapter four we learned that over an unfathomable time period random processes generated the diverse array of chemical elements of our world and organic synthesis emerged from a carbon framework. We also discussed several possible sources of these organic compounds in the prebiotic earth.

The most likely next step in the progression toward life required these precursor molecules to interact in productive ways to create larger, more complex molecular structures. Biologists call these structures biomolecules. Scientists studying life's origins try to understand how these biomolecules were first formed and how they led to rudimentary self-replicating systems and ultimately to life itself.

Because some believe it is impossible to trace life to its ultimate origins, it seems appropriate to ask whether science is adequately equipped to accomplish this feat. In my view the answer is, not yet. Even though many living organisms of today share common molecular pathways and superstructures, undeniable facts which suggest common origins, life is always changing. These changes lead to complex, overlapping, and integrated layers of organization at every level of life, which creates enormous barriers to full understanding. As a further complication, some of the earliest molecular pathways and structures probably became extinct millions of years ago.

But obstacles like these do not discourage scientists. They have a profound belief, based upon experience, that the physical world will ultimately make sense. Therefore, just as a skilled detective pieces together the various elements of a crime scene to recreate past events, modern scientists are using the growing wealth of scientific information to knit together a relatively coherent picture of how life on earth developed.

So the stage is set, and the players are in place. We are now ready to explore the next step toward the single most magnificent miracle of all—the creation of life.

The Fundamental Unit of Life—Living Cells

Every living thing is composed of dynamic structures called cells. Scientists are discovering that the best way to understand life is by investigating the cell's chemistry. Using this frame of reference, we would predict the chemistry of earth's earliest cells to have been relatively simple compared to the highly sophisticated cells seen today. For example, a human cell contains thousands of biochemical molecules interacting in a coordinated fashion within the confines of a cell membrane. Certainly, the first living cells of earth were much less complex.

The primary purpose of a cell's membrane is to segregate the cell from its external environment: It keeps valuable molecules in and unwanted molecules out. This function is so critical that if the integrity of a cell's membrane is compromised, the cell immediately dies. The fact that virtually every living form that has ever been observed, from bacteria to human beings, are either cells or made up of cells, and that these living organisms show clear progression in terms of their internal chemical complexity, suggests that the first life on earth was probably an extremely simple cell.

However, before this first rudimentary cell could arrive on the scene, the prebiotic chemical precursor molecules needed time to assemble, organize, and sort themselves out. These molecular assemblies, the biomolecules, were (and are) essential for life. A two-step synthetic process would first accumulate, and then select, the most useful biomolecules, while ignoring all others.

The Ingredients of Life—Biomolecules

Biomolecules logically organize into four distinct groups based on their chemical structure and corresponding biological functions.

These molecules provide the fundamental framework upon which all life is based. Therefore, it seems likely their presence was necessary to create the first life. The four major biomolecule groups are listed here.

- Proteins
- Carbohydrates (sometimes called sugars or polysaccharides)
- Lipids (fats)
- Nucleic acids (DNA and ribonucleic acid [RNA])

TABLE 5.1	
BIOMOLECULE GROUP	FUNCTIONAL ROLES
Proteins	Enzymes
	Carrier Proteins
	Antibodies
Carbohydrates	Energy Reserve/Storage
(Sugars and Polysaccharides)	Cells Receptors
	Plant Structure
Lipids (Fats)	Energy Storage
	Membrane Structure of Cells
Nucleic Acids (RNA and DNA)	Genetic Information
	Mutation/Variability
	Enzymes
	Information Transfer

Although each biomolecule group performs vital functions in living organisms, proteins and nucleic acids are arguably the most critical components to the initiation of life. For this reason, these molecules deserve closer attention.

Proteins form by linking amino acids into a linear chain, or polymer. As shown in Table 5.1, proteins have many functions.

Enzymes catalyze (accelerate) chemical reactions in the cell; transport proteins carry useful materials across the cell membrane; and antibodies protect the body from harmful germs. Nucleic acids are also polymers, but with a different chemical makeup. They are assembled from four chemical bases called nucleotides, and their primary role is to carry the cell's genetic information in a form similar to a binary computer code of zeros and ones.

How might these important molecules form in a prebiotic world? The following examples illustrate how scientists approach this problem.

Prebiotic Protein Synthesis

Sydney Fox at the University of Miami was one of the first scientists to successfully model prebiotic protein synthesis.[1] In his experiments, polymers of several hundred amino acids formed when a mixture of amino acids was dissolved in water and heated. These polymers were called proteinoids rather than proteins because they possessed some unusual amino acid linkages compared to typical proteins of today.

The discovery of proteinoids intrigued many scientists, especially when Fox's studies revealed that some proteinoids showed biological activity: They functioned as enzymes and catalyzed other chemical reactions. Although the catalytic efficiency of these proteinoids was lower than in the enzymes of contemporary living cells, the extraordinary results confirmed that prebiotic protein formation was feasible and may have played a key role in the first life assemblies.

Fox also made another intriguing observation. Although twenty different amino acids were included in the reaction pool, the incorporation of amino acids into the proteinoid chain was not entirely random. In other words, a built-in selection mechanism seemed to favor inclusion of certain amino acids over others. This finding is significant because it demonstrates once again that under certain circumstances, predictably random processes in the natural world may actually behave in non-random ways.

Prebiotic Nucleic Acid Synthesis (RNA)

Understanding the formation of nucleic acid chains under simulated prebiotic conditions presents two major challenges. One is to identify how the nucleotides physically linked as they formed larger nucleic acid polymers. The second challenge is discovering a copying mechanism that faithfully reproduces nucleic acid polymers after they have formed—a characteristic common to all life today.

Scientists use a variety of approaches to understand how these processes may have occurred on a prebiotic earth. One of the most intriguing studies was done by James Ferris at the Rensselaer Polytechnic Institute and reported in 1996.[2] Ferris and his colleagues demonstrated that nucleic acid chains up to fifty nucleotide units in length would form on a matrix of common montmorillonite clay, a matrix presumed present on the prebiotic ocean floor. The clay functions to concentrate the molecules on its surface and also acts as a mineral catalyst, encouraging the linking of nucleotides to proceed in a timely fashion.

Another intriguing observation is that the clay shows binding affinity for the nucleic acid polymers that are formed. This observation gave scientists the opportunity to explore the possibility of "template-directed" reproduction for nucleic acids, the method all living cells use today. In template-directed replication, new nucleic acid polymers are constructed using an existing nucleotide sequence as a guide—a primitive form of reproduction. Successful template-directed RNA formation in this system was also reported in 1996.[3]

Alternative models explaining how early proteins and nucleic acids assembled on the prebiotic planet have also been proposed, and some of these ideas are quite provocative. Gunter Wachtershauser, a German organic chemist, and his associates postulate that the whole process occurred on iron pyrite crystals next to volcanic vents in the ocean.[4] The tantalizing feature of this model is that preformed organic molecules (amino acids, sugars, etc.) are not initially required to start the process. The complete system is constructed using carbon dioxide to create organic precursors, which are then assembled directly into a growing web of molecular interactions. Although this model is relatively new and has not undergone extensive testing, it is tantalizing because it is consistent with the observation that some of the oldest and simplest known living cells (Archaebacteria) exist in such ocean vent environments.[5-7]

In summary, under laboratory conditions, scientists have synthesized both proteins and nucleic acids from their chemical precursors. It is important to remember, however, that although these findings tell us how prebiotic synthesis *could* occur on the planet, no one knows whether the conditions used for these experiments represent the real conditions of the prebiotic world. We simply can not go back in time and observe events as they unfolded. Therefore, our knowledge and understanding of these processes will always be incomplete.

Scientists face another perplexing problem: Laboratory experiments to synthesize proteins do not reveal how such processes are guided, even though guidance processes are essential to life today. In the prebiotic world, the unguided assembly of amino acids would likely create a whole potpourri of randomly assembled proteins. Proteins made in this manner would certainly not be expected to behave in useful ways. Without specific guidance or an effective selection mechanism to identify and select the rare functional proteins, it seems extremely unlikely that life could ever materialize from the non-living.

Scientists have ideas about this issue, but gaps in our understanding make definitive conclusions regarding precise mechanisms difficult. Nevertheless, we *do know* from the fossil record that simple living cells mysteriously appeared on earth over 3.5 billion years ago. This well documented knowledge *must* be incorporated into any credible discussion of the development of life. Two different explanations might account for the appearance of these early cells: A purposeful Designer—a God who instantaneously and supernaturally called these guidance systems and living cells into existence—or a process of random synthesis and selection which, given adequate time and appropriate conditions, worked *in equally miraculous ways* to create the first life. In this second scenario, the random assembly of specialized molecules, followed by the preferential selection of the most valuable variants, spark the whole sequence of creative events ultimately leading to the first living cell on the planet—a very early rendition of random design.

While this description of life's beginnings obviously oversimplifies an incredibly elaborate process, it is important because it establishes a logical connection to what we know of modern cell structure and function.

One other point is particularly noteworthy. As the principles related to the origin of life are evaluated, the concepts of formation and selection will often be analyzed and discussed individually. However, in real life we must be careful to remember that these processes are not easily disconnected. They are linked together in an intricate web, occurring automatically, simultaneously, and continuously, in every living thing.

Natural Selection

All life uniformly displays a system of selection or sorting—a process that provides overall direction to synthesis reactions. Modern science refers to this strategy as "natural selection." Typically, large repertoires of biological starting material, or precursors, form from simpler substances. The best candidates are then selected to accomplish specific biological tasks. Selection regimens of this sort are common in everyday life. For example, when shopping for a lawn mower you might evaluate five different mowers before taking one home. You would probably choose a push mower for a small yard, but a tractor mower might be more appropriate for a ten-acre sprawl. Your decision would be based on price, quality, and your specific mowing needs. In a very real sense, biological selection functions in a similar manner. It is an unemotional, yet extraordinarily effective decision-making system.

Natural selection may bring to mind the concept of evolution among living things. This is certainly a valid association. Evolution and natural selection are central features of all biology. Of course, natural selection in biology is not a conscious process like selecting a lawn mower, but it is still an important built-in quality of nature, occurring continuously and automatically, and with life-giving results. In addition, scientists recognize that natural selection does not occur just in larger living plants and animals. It also happens at the invisible molecular level. Indeed, the molecules composing the basic constructs of life appear to have miraculously survived multitudes of rigorous selection routines.

Natural Selection at the Molecular Level

When different molecules are mixed together in water, each behaves in a unique manner based on its electrical charge, size, ability to dissolve in water (solubility), and other properties. For example, sugars and salts, because of their charge, dissolve quickly and easily in aqueous solutions, but oils do not. In this same solution, some molecules might maintain distinctive identities, while others would quickly connect with their neighbors to form more complex assemblies.

A fully functioning selection process chooses molecules with the most beneficial combinations of characteristics (stability, solubility, or tendency to interact with neighbors) to accomplish the purpose at hand. For the first biological molecules on earth, the primary selection screen may have been stability in water—the ability to survive. Using this criterion, the most stable molecules—perhaps amino acids or simple proteins—would preferentially accumulate. Once these stable molecules attained critical concentrations, another logical selection regimen would emerge and build on the first, using the most stable molecules to successfully interact with one another, producing yet larger and more complex organized structure.

On rare occasions, a newly formed complex structure might even acquire a useful biological function, such as the capacity to catalyze other synthetic reactions. In addition, interacting molecules could converge to form large visible biological structures. A very simple demonstration of this process can be easily observed by combining a mixture of fatty acids with water and vigorously agitating. Under these conditions, the molecules seem to magically assemble into organized spherical structures called liposomes. In appearance and properties, these liposomes bear remarkable resemblances to living cells of today.

Other selection criteria may have also helped determine which original building block molecules would be used to initiate life. For example, scientists know amino acids, the primary component of proteins, can exist in nature as one of two chemical forms. In simple terms we designate these two forms as either right or left-handed. Both types are relatively stable, but modern proteins contain only the left-handed forms.

What selection mechanisms could account for this observation? Randomness may have played a role. The first protein synthesizing enzymes may, by chance, have simply preferred left-handed amino acids to the right-handed ones: Certainly, every biologist knows that enzymes routinely possess this type of fine discriminating power. However, regardless of the precise mechanism, once the decision was made to incorporate only left-handed amino acids into the initial scaffolding of life, every biological structure that followed would necessarily be built upon this foundation. We do know this particular decision occurred very early in the development of life because virtually all protein synthesizing enzymes in today's cells only use "lefties."

As in all frontiers of scientific study, scientists who research life's origins have many unanswered questions. However, some things really are well established. We know that selection strategies are real and vital ingredients of life. But to truly understand natural selection in living organisms, we must view it from the proper perspective. The actual process is incredibly slow—nearly imperceptible during a short time span. Therefore, we can only follow the effects of variation and natural selection in biology over extremely long time periods—often much greater than the human lifespan.

One additional feature of natural selection merits special note: Natural selection is not a recent development. It functioned in our world long before Charles Darwin's 1859 publication, *The Origin of Species*. As ancient as the earth itself, natural selection is a straightforward and methodical process, ensuring that every new molecular species receives a complete and thorough evaluation of its potential usefulness in the overall scheme of life. There is no reasonable basis for attaching arbitrary value judgments to the concept. It is neither good nor bad. It is just the way things are—and apparently the way they have always been.

Immense obstacles and an enormous number of variables impede our efforts to understand how life began on our planet. After decades of study, the simple fact is that no one knows precisely how early organic molecules came together to accomplish this miraculous feat. Despite these challenges, we do recognize two vital features of early life: The formation of essential biomolecules, and the natural selection and evolution of these life-giving structures.

But for living things, the natural selection process is only as good as the starting materials. Therefore, whether considering molecules or living cells, natural selection works best when a great number and variety of precursors are available to produce successful pathways of biological synthesis.

Magnificent Molecular Micro-Machines

Random Assemblies
Lead to Life-Giving Form

6

To display even the most rudimentary characteristics of life, the first living cells must have already possessed remarkable physical structure. This chapter introduces some of the most essential components of living organisms—the fundamental building blocks of all life.

Automobiles are systematically assembled from a multitude of specialized components that impart desirable characteristics and functions to each car. In a like manner, living cells are also created from the systematic assembly of individual components. As reviewed in chapter five, the cellular components of life—the biomolecules—perform a mind-boggling array of critical activities for the cell. Each biomolecule, whether a protein, lipid, polysaccharide, or nucleic acid, has a unique chemical makeup that finds expression in a specialized shape or conformation. This unique conformation imparts to the molecule a one-of-a-kind capacity to carry out important cellular tasks. In a sense, each biomolecule is endowed with a distinctive individual personality. This foundational principle of biology can be expressed in the following statement: *Biological structure determines the corresponding life-giving function.*

This concept is illustrated by the tools of everyday life. Picture a fork, a shovel, or a lawn mower. The shape (structure) of these garden tools is perfectly suited to their function. The main differences between garden tools and the tools of cells are that biomolecular tools of cells are significantly more fragile, highly specialized, incredibly small, and function only within the aqueous (water) environment of a cell.

A classic example is the protein hormone insulin, a vital molecule that enables the human body to maintain a healthy state. Insulin binds to a variety of body cells, signaling these cells to absorb glucose from the blood. If an individual has defective or deficient insulin, the signaling process fails to perform properly resulting in a disease state called diabetes mellitus. The insulin molecule is exquisitely small: When suspended in the liquid plasma of the blood, it is less than 5 nanometers, or 0.000000005 meters, in diameter. In contrast, the average small garden pea is about 10 millimeters, or just under one-half inch in diameter.

To visualize these molecules in the context of a living cell, consider the following: If an insulin molecule were enlarged to the size of a garden pea and the pea size adjusted by a corresponding factor, the pea would stretch nearly 6 miles across. Now, picture this 6-mile wide pea (representing the insulin protein) floating within an enclosed spherical membrane of water 36,000 miles in diameter (the earth's diameter is 7,918 miles). This creates a comparable mental image of a single protein floating within a living cell. Small molecules indeed!

Proteins

Although each biomolecule group is essential to cell survival, the most crucial group is the proteins. Structurally, proteins are linear connected assemblies of up to twenty different amino acids. These amino acids, resembling colored beads on a string, prescribe an exact ordered sequence and impart distinctive chemical characteristics to each protein.

The chemical interactions of the amino acids within these chains create individual proteins with incredibly precise three-dimensional folding patterns, or shapes. In addition, the consistent uniform nature of these interactions ensures that multiple molecules of a particular protein will always have identical amino acid sequences, three-dimensional shapes, and corresponding biological functions. Figure 6.1 illustrates this concept.

The red blood cell protein hemoglobin provides another excellent example of protein structure. Its three-dimensional folding pattern allows it to bind oxygen molecules and carry them to all parts of the body. Hemoglobin contains 287 amino acids organized

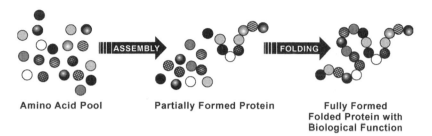

Figure 6.1   Protein Formation

in a precise linear array. If a scientist were to analyze the blood of a person and check the identity of the 126th amino acid in each hemoglobin protein, the same amino acid would always be found in that position. Maintaining the proper amino acid sequences in proteins is an extremely high priority for cells, which would suggest that a protein's function is fragile and easily disrupted by small changes. Indeed, this is true: Most proteins are severely and negatively impacted by even small changes in their structure, and damaged proteins can lead to severe problems within the host cell or organism.

For example, the disease sickle-cell anemia is precipitated by a change in only one amino acid out of 287 in the hemoglobin protein. The third amino acid in the protein chain, glutamic acid, is replaced by the amino acid valine. This relatively subtle change causes hemoglobin molecules and red blood cells to assume distorted shapes. And although this change might seem minor, the overall effects can be life threatening: Hemoglobin loses the ability to effectively distribute oxygen to the body's cells.

For most proteins, all twenty amino acids are represented in various combinations in the molecule. However, other proteins do not use all twenty. Indeed, some of the simplest proteins contain only eight different amino acids. This fact tells us that even very simple proteins can exhibit meaningful biological function, and that the earliest cellular proteins could easily have been constructed from a much more limited repertoire of amino acids than modern proteins. Again, we see the pattern of life progressively developing from simple to more complex structures.

But what are proteins, really? Practically speaking, most people think of proteins as important nutritional substances. Of course, this is true. Everyone knows that proteins are important components of a balanced diet, but in the context of a living cell, proteins are much more. They are elegant molecular micro-machines—the workhorses of the cell—the guys who get things done. And in this role, proteins are essential to life.

More specifically, some proteins function as enzymes—biological protein catalysts that spark synthetic reactions and promote changes in other large biomolecules. The speed of enzyme-catalyzed reactions is almost unimaginable, in some cases modifying over 1,000 molecules per second. The extraordinary speed and specificity of enzymes are crucial to our survival: Without enzymes, the biochemical reactions within our cells would simply not take place fast enough to sustain life.

Another group of important proteins are the binding proteins. In a very real sense, the language of life is touch and these biomolecules establish elaborate cellular communication systems as they bind with exquisite precision to other molecules and important cell components. Yet other proteins are architectural proteins, participating in the formation of an intricate, delicate, and majestic microscopic matrix within the cells and tissues of living things. High magnification microscopes pull this amazing and grand architecture into full view for scientists to see. And when these molecular palaces are visualized following appropriate staining procedures, the beauty and magnificence is simply beyond description.

Figure 6.2 summarizes a few important functions of proteins.

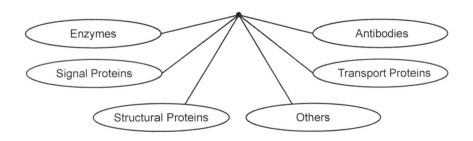

Figure 6.2   Protein Functions

Taken together, the specialized functions of a cell's proteins and the hyper-speed interactions of these and thousands of other bio-molecules impart to cells the most astounding characteristics of all—the characteristics of life. This central concept can now be stated in a more general manner: *A living cell is the product of the distinctive proteins it makes.* Hence, a human kidney cell is a kidney cell because of its exceptional protein combinations. Likewise, brain cells, plant cells, bacterial cells, and the cells of every living creature are what they are because of their peculiar proteins.

Figure 6.3 illustrates this concept by comparing nerve cells with skin cells. You will note that while the cells share some proteins, other proteins occur exclusively on just one cell type. The practical consequence of this observation is that by adding, deleting, or changing one or more proteins within a cell, the fundamental identity of the cell can be modified. This understanding drives modern genetic engineering techniques and biotechnology. By changing one gene in the corn plant to produce a single new protein, scientists render the plant resistant to certain insect pests. On the medical front, replacing a defective protein with a normal version,

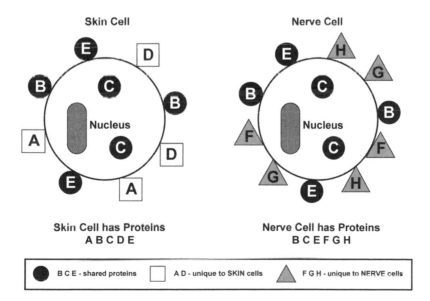

Figure 6.3   A Cell Is the Product of its Proteins

physicians will soon be able to treat diseases such as hemophilia, immune disorders, and cancer.

The idea that all living things are a reflection of their proteins has extraordinary ramifications for the very nature of life. A seemingly limitless number of life forms have inhabited our planet over billions of years. Each organism, both past and present, has resulted from different combinations of the twenty amino acids that comprise cell proteins.

At first glance, it would seem impossible to generate such incredible diversity from such a small pool of amino acid building blocks. However, in living organisms where random design has been effectively operating for billions of years, the task is actually quite simple.

If we think of amino acids as letters in a life-giving code, much like the 26 letters of the English alphabet, I think we can glimpse the possibilities. How many one-letter combinations will the 26-letter alphabet produce? The obvious answer is 26^1, or 26. For two letter words, the theoretical possibility rockets to 26^2, or 676. For three letter words, 26^3, or 17,576, and so on. The same principle applies to protein construction. Proteins come in many different sizes, but a mid-sized protein is typically about 100 amino acids in length. Therefore, a chain this length could theoretically generate 20^{100} different amino acid combinations, or 20^{100} different functional proteins. The magnitude of this number is mind-numbing, calculating out to the number one followed by 130 zeros. To mathematicians, this is more than a google (the number one with 100 trailing zeros). For the rest of us regular people, it is virtually infinite. Remember the calendar date of one billion minutes ago from our previous discussion? One billion is the number one with *only* nine trailing zeros.

The mathematics behind these structure/function relationships is complicated, yet also elegantly simple. Using combinatorial mathematics, biology routinely accomplishes mind-boggling synthetic feats. For our discussions of life, the immediate consequence is crystal clear: Assembled appropriately, just twenty amino acid molecules have boundless potential.

The ultimate outcome? *An infinite number of possible protein struc-tures provide an infinite number of possible protein functions, an infinite number of possible cell types, and an infinite number of different life forms.*

This incredibly productive method for creating diversity is another example of random design. When the largest number of possibilities is made available, the best solutions eventually emerge from the mix. Suitable mechanisms then select molecules best equipped for the cell's task. This mechanism appears to be natural selection, or something akin to it.

I must confess, these processes never cease to amaze me. But while we may find them amazing, the Random Designer is not the least bit astonished. Unlimited potential is His very nature, and random design is part of His process and plan. He beckons us to come closer and learn more.

Instructions for Life
The Genetic Code Is Set

7

Genetic Information—DNA and RNA

As we have seen, the cell's proteins prescribe the physical characteristics of every living cell. This understanding raises the question of how cells successfully construct the precise proteins needed to carry out their individual life-giving functions. The answer is that the cell's proteins are produced according to a precise set of instructions that have direct relationships with another group of important biomolecules called the nucleic acids—DNA and RNA. These molecules thus establish the blueprint for life. The basic structure of DNA parallels the linear amino acid structure of proteins in many ways. The difference is that proteins use twenty amino acids to construct their structure, whereas in DNA just four chemical subunits, or nucleotides, are sufficient. These nucleotides, adenine, guanine, cytosine, and thymine (A,G,C,T) link together in an ordered sequence. And as we shall see shortly, this sequence prescribes the essential protein elements of all life.

While the amino acids of proteins seem to form quite easily under prebiotic conditions, demonstrating how the four nucleotides originated on earth is more difficult. Nevertheless, scientists actively researching this subject believe nucleotide molecules were—like amino acids—created by prebiotic organic synthesis reactions available at the time. After their formation, the nucleotides would then be available to assemble into polymers of RNA and DNA.

In modern cells, DNA is organized into long linear strands called chromosomes. Nestled within the base sequences of these chromosomes is a complex, but coherent, blueprint for each and every living cell. The sheer volume of life-giving information packaged within the cell's chromosomes is astronomical. Consider that the DNA within one human cell contains over six billion chemical bases in a precise and ordered array—enough letters to fill a book of four million pages. If one could take all forty-six chromosomes from each of the cells of one human being, stretch the DNA in these chromosomes to their full length, and lay them end to end, these 75 trillion cells would contain enough DNA to form a continuous chain reaching to the sun and back more than 500 times. (Figure 7.1) Now that is a lot of information! Imagine the incredible packing ratios needed to fit all this genetic code inside one human body.

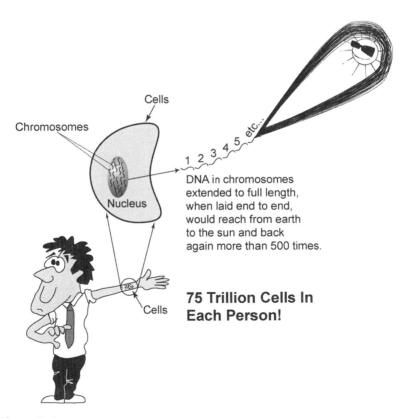

Cells

Chromosomes

Nucleus

DNA in chromosomes extended to full length, when laid end to end, would reach from earth to the sun and back again more than 500 times.

Cells

75 Trillion Cells In Each Person!

Figure 7.1

Genes Contain the Secrets of Life

The cell's chromosomes, delicately wound coils of DNA, are found tightly packed into the cell's nucleus. Spaced intermittently within the cell's chromosomes, scientists find specialized stretches of nucleotide bases. These segments are called genes. Surprisingly, only about 1% of the nucleotide bases within the chromosome actually constitute coding genes. This discovery, that nearly 99% of the DNA is junk, seeming to have no protein coding function, has puzzled scientists for many years. Nonetheless, the genes are of paramount importance for the cell because they contain the instructions for producing every protein.

Recall from the last chapter that a cell is the product of the proteins it makes. Therefore, since instructions for making the cell's proteins come from the genes, it is easy to see a direct link between genes and proteins. The unique nucleotide base sequence of each gene prescribes a precise amino acid sequence in the resulting protein. The ordered assembly of these amino acids and their interactions with each other directly lead to the protein's distinctive three-dimensional shape and corresponding function. (Figure 7.2) This basic understanding of gene/protein correspondence leads to an expanded cell premise: *A cell is the product of the proteins it makes, and the proteins a particular cell makes are a direct reflection of the genes present in its chromosomes.*

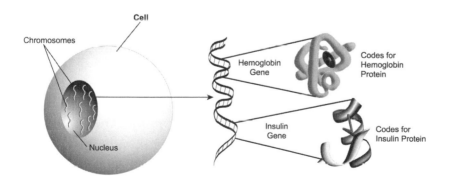

Figure 7.2 Information Flow—Gene to Protein

From this premise, it follows that living cells must rigorously maintain the integrity of their nucleotide base sequence: Its genetic information must be preserved. However, scientists find that each time a cell reproduces itself, there is the potential for errors in copying the DNA to occur. Therefore, the DNA copying machinery must perform its assignment with a high degree of fidelity to minimize mistakes and ensure that the daughter cells will survive and function properly. Even single nucleotide base modifications within a gene can change the amino acid sequence, causing dramatic alterations to the protein's specialized structure and function. Altering a gene sequence responsible for directing the production of an essential protein may even lead to the cell's death. Even more significantly, a single damaged cell sometimes extends its harmful effects to the whole organism. Severe physical or developmental problems and even death may ensue. For example, altering just one critical nucleotide base within an important growth regulation gene changes the protein product sufficiently to convert this otherwise normal cell into a malignant cancer.

Imagine! Human beings have over six billion nucleotide chemical bases in each cell and altering just one of these bases can produce incredibly sobering consequences. We are wonderfully complex, yet also remarkably fragile!

How are living beings, including humans, able to derive such precise and meaningful information from just four chemical bases? Once again, the random design principle plays an important role. Compare it to Morse code, which interprets various combinations of dots and dashes as letters of the alphabet. For example, dash, dash, dot equals G; dash, dash, dash equals O; and dash, dot, dot stands for D. Arranged properly, just two basic symbols can represent the complete English alphabet, forming meaningful words that can be strung together into larger concepts.

In the same way, different combinations of a gene's four chemical bases provide a cellular code prescribing which sequence of amino acids (protein) is produced. The fully assembled proteins then interact to construct higher-level cell function. But to use the code for making a protein, the cell must decipher the language of the four chemical bases.

A cell is the product of the proteins it makes, and the proteins a particular cell makes are a direct reflection of the genes present in its chromosomes.

Fortunately, scientists have completely worked out the molecular details of this genetic coding and deciphering system. The code is expressed as a series of three-letter words, with each code word specifying one of the twenty unique amino acids found in proteins. For example, just as dash, dash, dot equals G in Morse code, the triplet chemical bases AAA, GTC, and CAG are code words for the amino acids phenylalanine, glutamine, and valine respectively. The molecular machinery that guides this system maintains the critical one-to-one relationship between the coded instructions of the gene and the corresponding protein that results from the expression of this gene.

Remember, a cell is the product of the proteins it makes, and proteins are a consequence of the genes within a particular cell. Hence, this system establishes a productive platform upon which biological organisms can survive and thrive. But this platform, as it exists today, did not easily materialize on its own. There is yet another unresolved mystery that baffles scientists.

In modern cells, genes are required to direct the synthesis of proteins in a cell, but it turns out that some of the products of these genes are specialized proteins that are themselves required to synthesize and maintain the embedded genes of DNA. It is a classic "chicken-egg" dilemma: Genes are needed to make proteins and proteins are needed to make genes. So which came first? Or did this interdependence develop together?

Honestly, this is a difficult question. Unless God supernaturally intervened, instantaneously establishing this system from nothing, then it had to be constructed one step at a time, first from simple components, then into more complex interacting systems.

A book of this nature cannot possibly delineate all the scientific evidence regarding this dilemma. Scientists continuously grapple with these and other difficult questions. And although many observations within biology strongly point toward a stepwise and interdependent development scheme, definitive conclusions must await further study. Even the most knowledgeable scientists in this field face a deluge of questions that seem beyond our present capacity to comprehend. Here are a few that come to mind:

- What precise conditions were required to form a living and reproducing cell?
- How did the process begin?
- Which molecular assemblies came first—nucleic acids or proteins?
- What specialized functions were most critical to continue the building and assembly process?
- How did the apparently crucial process of protein-nucleic acid recognition and interdependence develop in simple and then modern cells?

Modern biology primarily investigates the chemistry of living cells. The picture that is emerging indicates that proteins and nucleic acids were important components of the early world and became enclosed within a membrane-like cell structure at a very early stage. Based upon this information, scientists believe simple proteins formed from amino acids in a primitive prebiotic (pre-life) milieu. A similar image emerges for the formation of simple nucleic acid chains. It does not require a huge leap of faith to postulate that prebiotic proteins or nucleic acids, acting as enzymes, catalyzed the formation of increasingly more complex biological organization or served as structural components within the confines of a cell. In this cellular state, the essential components of life (proteins, nucleic acids, sugars, and lipids) could actually coexist in adequate concentrations to intermingle and communicate productively. This is not yet life, but it is getting close to it.

Realistically, the quest to understand every aspect regarding the formation of earth's very first cell may be one of the most difficult and challenging tasks of all time for biology. Despite the challenge, modern scientific investigation has accumulated many interesting and surprising pieces of life's puzzle. And although the picture is far from complete, a large number of these pieces fit together into a coherent and compelling framework. Therefore, it seems naive to ignore or discount the beautiful canvas materializing right before our eyes as our understanding of biology and our physical origins expands.

So how many successes would be necessary to establish stable life on a prebiotic planet? A modern understanding of how biology works at the molecular/cellular level leads to the conclusion that this seemingly difficult question may actually have a very simple answer: Just one cell may have been sufficient. And while realistically, the complete details regarding the origin of this first cell will probably never be fully deciphered or understood, once the first replicating cell arrived on the scene, it is relatively easy for scientists to construct a coherent paradigm for the formation of all living organisms from this one cell.

Imagine—a single progenitor (parent) cell serving as the foundation for all living cells and every life form that has ever existed. It seems incredible to me. Some people would even call it a miracle. Others simply say it is unbelievable. But the Random Designer says that this grand drama was simply an early part of the magnificent plan designed to accomplish His purposes.

Trial and Error—or Is It Trial and Success?

A Difficult Question with a Difficult Answer

8

Despite valiant attempts to reconstruct a hypothetical scenario surrounding the first life on our planet, many questions remain unanswered. Fortunately for mankind, the plausibility of such a life-creating event does not hinge on our ability to understand its precise mechanisms: Just because something is difficult to understand does not make it impossible. In fact, fossil, chemical, and other scientific evidence overwhelmingly tells of an astonishing event occurring one day billions of years ago, early in our planet's history: The first simple cell was formed on earth, apparently constructed from the immense available resources of the prebiotic planet.

This cell would certainly have possessed many astonishing features, including a rudimentary capacity for self-duplication. Consistent with the observation that many common biochemical mechanisms and biological structures are uniformly represented in all living organisms from the most simple to most complex, and that increasing biological diversity and complexity follow a geologically verifiable time line, it appears that all life on our planet developed from this single primordial cell. This understanding, along with several other scientific principles, establishes the essential biological framework for a discussion of random design.

Prior to this discussion, however, a key premise concerning our most fundamental concepts of God and how life operates in our world must be considered.

Chapter five introduced the notion of synthesis and selection in biological systems—a very simple form of random design. When considering this idea at the level of biological molecules, simple cells, or less developed organisms, the random design principle is not difficult to comprehend and embrace. The thought of creating large numbers of precursors, then selecting those best suited for a particular function, seems to be exquisitely effective. Such a positive selection scheme even seems American! In business or scientific jargon, it is a variation on survival of the fittest—or he who has the best mousetrap wins.

The random design concept, then, is a real and integral principle that influences our lives in many ways. Indeed, as the story unfolds I believe you will see that the random design model is also a wonderful, life-generating plan, possessing boundless creative potential. Most importantly, random design processes can actually be tapped and used to fuel the perpetual growth and development of living organisms.

However, the random design concept also contains an unattractive side: By its very nature, random design is an exclusive process. Implicit in this statement is the troublesome reality that many candidates will lack adequate attributes or value to be selected for inclusion or survival.

Once again, when we consider the most basic molecules that are a part of life, this is not much of an issue. However, when the rule is applied to higher organisms it becomes a more serious and emotionally ponderous proposition. It morphs from an apparently benign and distant application of a neutral scientific concept into a vivid reality. And when this rule is fully assigned to the very highest forms of life, including humans, the ramifications become enormous and intensely personal. In fact, it literally becomes a matter of life or death.

Such an exclusionary idea may actually seem rather harsh, but I must be honest with you: Even this description does not convey the full impact of random design. In a very real sense, it is not only harsh and cruel; in many ways it is downright brutal. But regardless of how we humans interpret it, this exclusionary principle cannot be legitimately dismissed. It is soberingly real and verifiable in multitudes of everyday life situations.

Human beings justifiably take great pride in positive personal values and high moral standards. Indeed, these values may be the most important element that sets us apart from other living creatures. And a shared set of values is good for humanity. One concept that is nearly universal is the value of life itself, particularly human life. Consequently, attempting to reconcile our shared values with the random design concept raises a potential problem: Many people simply cannot bring themselves to embrace the full exclusionary implications of the random design model when applied to human beings, especially when it results in, and perhaps even dictates, physical suffering and death.

Consistent Rules of Life

Are human beings really subject to the same rules of biological selection as all other biological entities? Are we willing to accept the undeniable fact that we are really and truly *fully* biological? Individually, the honest and thoughtful responses to these questions carry with them tremendous implications for how life is viewed and lived.

Of course many individuals will say that we are fully biological, but also much more. At a later point in this book, it will become apparent that I strongly agree. However, if this belief is extrapolated forward to the point of suggesting that we are somehow above fundamental biological rules of existence, it has gone too far.

It seems to me that many people do in fact cling to such an idea, either consciously or subconsciously. Their views are elaborated in a manner something like this: "The laws of biochemistry, genetics, evolution, and selection are okay for simple life forms, but do not even speak to me about human evolution!"

People of certain religious convictions might even claim these ideas cannot possibly be true because, according to their interpretation, they are not scriptural. In spite of such objections, the more we learn about life, the more we are compelled to face the stark and glaring truth. Random design applies at *every* level of life, from the simple to the most complex—including our very own. Humans cannot avoid the inefficiency, hardships, pain, and physical death that are a product of the random design paradigm and life itself. We are full and complete participants.

Of course, there are many possible responses to these ideas. We can deny the random design concept. We can redefine it. We can ignore it. We can attack it. We can even pretend it will go away. But it never goes away. It has always been with us, and the overwhelming scientific evidence indicates that it is here to stay. A trail of death and destruction follows earth's history from the beginning of time up to this very moment. And as stunning and difficult as this concept may be, random design appears to be a uniform and consistent product of the hand of God.

Is it possible to view such an uncomfortable and difficult concept in a positive light? I believe the answer to this question is a resounding "Yes!" But we must be willing to examine the issue closely and see the concept within a larger framework. For in doing so, we find the random design concept also contains many beneficial aspects.

Within the parameters of His natural laws, the Random Designer does not limit His options. He is apparently willing to try all possibilities in order to accomplish His predetermined purposes.

On the surface, such an approach might appear grossly inefficient and unproductive. It guarantees that most tested possibilities, and the living beings that result, will ultimately fail to be integrated into the larger scheme of life. However, the extreme irony of this thought is that *random design may be the only way to truly maximize biological productivity and ensure ultimate success. It guarantees that virtually every possible solution will be generated and also checked.* Thus failure, as generally defined, is apparently a distinctive part of the Random Designer's creative processes.

The ramifications of this observation are vividly apparent and may be troublesome for those who have been taught from an early age that God cannot be associated with negative and disorderly processes. And He certainly could not be connected in any way to the idea of failure. For these people, associating God with exclusion, destruction, or death is simply unthinkable. And this is where we encounter the dilemma: New discoveries that routinely arise from science and biology often create significant challenges for those who wish to reconcile their religious convictions with physical reality.

New Definitions of Success

When the scientific evidence is honestly examined in concert with a wealth of personal human experiences, the inescapable conclusion is that the Random Designer must define success and failure differently than humans.

Words like randomness and failure generally carry unfavorable connotations. But the Random Designer appears to hold a different view. He seems quite comfortable creating complex living beings using mechanisms that require uniformly high failure rates. In fact, these failure rates are so high that the successful formation of any complex entity, much less a living organism, would be expected to be an extremely *rare* event rather than the rule. *But to the Random Designer, real failure does not exist! A string of separate events that appears devastating from our perspective is not even a setback for Him.*

And while the improbable nature of some events makes them seem impossible to us, they become virtual certainties when an adequate number of opportunities are granted. For example, consider a particular biological development event in a group of cells— perhaps a mutation that improves a protein's function and maximizes the cell's growth potential. Suppose this mutation had a low probability of occurrence   say, one in a million. Practically speaking, we would probably assign the odds for improving the protein's function at nearly zero. After all, in most of life's situations one in a million odds is not very promising.

> But to the Random Designer, real failure simply does not exist! A string of separate events that appears devastating from our limited perspective is not even a setback for Him.

However, the study of complex cells and biological organisms does not support this conclusion. Of course, if the cells in this example had only one opportunity to improve, their chances would indeed be minimal. However, if the cells have 10 million chances to improve the protein, we would actually expect to see *ten* successful outcomes.

The realism and significance of this illustration should not be minimized: Large-scale trials of this sort are routine in biological systems. When given sufficient time and opportunity, extremely unlikely events in biology often become virtual certainties.

But do not forget the flip side. The success of the improved protein came at the expense of 9,999,990 failures. Therefore, when viewed in its entirety, these failures were a vital part of the ultimate success. Each failure identified one possibility that would not work, or at least one that did not perform as well as another.

Certainly, processes that result in failure, elimination, or death do not seem very efficient. Nor do they appear at first glance to embody any meaningful design potential. Yet despite apparent inefficiencies, elegant design clearly permeates all of biology. A vivid example is seen in the development of certain blood cells.

Human blood is composed of many different cell types. Most are red blood cells whose function is to carry oxygen and carbon dioxide back and forth from the lungs to various body tissues. Another important group of cells, the white blood cells, protect the body by recognizing and attacking infectious agents such as bacteria and viruses. Mature T cells are a specialized group of white blood cells programmed to aggressively attack infectious agents while leaving normal cells and tissues unharmed.

Tiny T cells begin as immature precursor cells. Each day of our lives, millions of these immature cells are created in our bone marrow and migrate via the blood to another specialized organ called the thymus gland. At this point the T cells possess no protective function; however within the thymus gland they are exposed to hormones and growth-enhancing substances that act as development signals. These signals encourage the cells to grow and mature into fully functioning T cells and acquire their full protective functions. Scientists who first examined the T cell maturation process in detail were surprised and baffled to discover glaring inefficiency within the development scheme. As the entering T cells progressed through the thymus, nearly 99% of them failed to mature successfully. Not only did they fail to mature, each of the unsuccessful cells died shortly thereafter. Only about 1% of the original T cells actually survived and developed their full potential.

From a limited understanding, this system appears quite wasteful: Millions of the T cells made within us each day are never used. In fact, those not used are proactively destroyed. However, scientists have learned that there is much more to this story. A positive effect and a vital purpose emerge from this massive killing.

The thymus gland has a specific task. (Figure 8.1) In addition to selecting and nurturing protective T cells, it must also identify any T cells that would harm the body and signal these cells to self-destruct. It does this by imposing a complicated and rigorous selection regimen upon each entering immature T cell. Thus, in an interesting

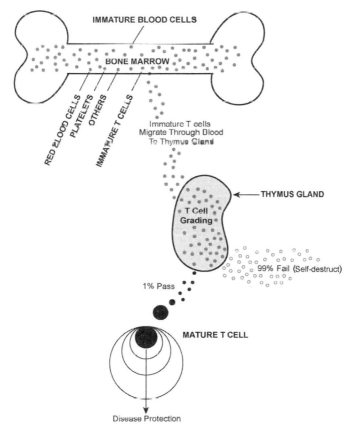

Figure 8.1   T Cell Formation

twist of irony, *this rigid selection protocol that destroys so many hopeful T cells is, in fact, crucial to our survival.* Those cells that would have insidiously attacked our bodies from within are systematically and mercilessly eliminated. In the final analysis, the complicated system of T cell development seems to be less than efficacious, but the results turn out to be nothing less than divine.

Failure Breeds Success

In the same way, the Random Designer apparently gives little thought to efficiency. And why should He? His resources are infinite. He apparently values quality over quantity. Human beings generally place a high value on efficiency, precision, and order. Accordingly, our personal concepts and descriptions relating to the character of God frequently follow similar lines. For this reason, some people may find it difficult to embrace a Creator who creates using something akin to 'trial and error'.

Fortunately, such uneasiness does not hamper the Random Designer. He resolutely presses on. He is intent upon His goals, regardless of mankind's views or acceptance of His mechanisms. He is evidently more concerned with final outcomes than with intermediate processes, nonproductive pathways, or the approval of one of His creatures. He is determined to find the best solutions to accomplish His grand plan.

In a very real sense then, failure abounds! Yet, emanating from the carnage that occurs at literally every level of biology, at least one, and sometimes several, productive pathways emerge. These pathways progressively establish structured and stable states among living organisms. As a consequence, each form of life acquires the potential to bridge life onward and upward to new levels of existence. This process, repeating over and over in an endless and infinite series of trials, propels life toward the Creator's ultimate purposes. Out of apparent chaos, unbelievable biological constructs spring forth.

Many other examples will be provided to show that random design is commonplace. In fact, it is absolutely essential to our survival. But for now it seems to me that if we genuinely wish to understand life and the Random Designer, it means acknowledging that things are not always warm and fuzzy. In fact, the Creator sometimes uses mechanisms that seem downright repulsive. But such a suggestion is not religious heresy or even cause for concern. Remember, our understanding and perspective is limited. We see only the present. The Random Designer has a vision far greater than ours. He sees a future and purpose extending well beyond what we can conceptualize at the present time.

So with randomness and chaos all around us, will we have the courage to trust Him? Will we have the necessary resolve to keep searching for Him when we fail to understand His ways—even if we discover they are hard, we do not especially like them, or they seem to be at odds with our religious traditions? Will we openly and honestly seek Him, even when, on occasion, we inevitably experience the real and deeply penetrating pain of human existence?

To these questions, as with questions of science, the Random Designer says, "Have faith: There is much more to learn!"

The Platform of Life

*Mutation, Natural Selection,
and Biological Development*

9

The three previous chapters highlighted several important points regarding living cells. First, specialized functions of biological molecules arise from their unique structure, and the rapid interactions between various molecules lead to this wonderful outcome called life.

The second point concerns the genes embedded within the base sequences of the DNA. Remember, living cells are essentially a direct consequence of the proteins they make, and the coded information contained within each gene is directly mirrored in the amino acid sequence of the corresponding protein. Therefore, this one-for-one relationship between DNA and proteins ultimately means that genetic information guides all life-giving activities of the cell. Any alteration in a gene produces a change in the corresponding protein and also in the cell's characteristics.

Third, the workings of biology are not always neat and tidy. Random processes, tremendous inefficiency, and even death are innately built into the very nature of living systems.

Throughout earth's history and against tremendous odds, biological molecules have interacted cooperatively to create novel and increasingly complex biological structure and function, as well as astonishing higher-level organization. The whole idea is another mysterious paradox. What seemingly improbable platform could possibly drive this determination and direction so routinely observed in biology? These final chapters of section I will address this question and complete the essential scientific foundation for understanding the physical nature of life. Once again we will see that biology utilizes randomness to maximum advantage as the means to overcome seemingly intractable obstacles.

Mutation and Natural Selection

The platform chosen by the Random Designer appears to be random mutation and subsequent selection. Most everyone will immediately recognize this platform as the process of evolution. Individuals (with their own particular gene variations) who acquire and accumulate positive changes experience a competitive survival advantage in future generations. Individuals with less desirable gene combinations find themselves at a selective biological disadvantage and tend to be discarded, or at least superseded, by those who possess genes that are more favorable.

As discussed in the previous chapter, in the context of living things, a synthesis/selection platform of this nature is frequently quite messy. In fact, it carries a predictable and relatively early death sentence for many of the participants. Because of this, the word mutation often conjures up ominous mental images of monsters, clones, disease, and death. But as with so many other media perceptions, these images are both unfortunate and unrealistic. A mutation is actually nothing more than an alteration in the chemical base coding sequence of DNA. Such an event does not automatically deserve a negative connotation: It is simply a change.

In reality, altered genetic information leads to three possible consequences: Damaging, beneficial, or neutral, depending on the specific effect the change conveys to the affected cell. While it is true that most mutations are harmful, even these observations may be skewed by our vantage point in time because mutational effects observed today act upon relatively modern and complex living organisms. *These organisms, having previously experienced countless rounds of mutation and natural selection over billions of years, are already highly developed and refined in their genetic organization. And this fact makes a huge difference in our perception.*

For example, suppose I own a finely engineered Swiss watch. What effect would a small, but totally random change have on this watch? Would the change cause improved or diminished function? I am sure you would agree that the random change *could* lead to improvement, but such an outcome would be highly unlikely. In the same way, because of the highly ordered and structured state existing within the cells, most random mutations lead to impaired function in living organisms.

Given this understanding, suppose 99.99999% of the random mutations in the genes of a cell or organism were harmful or lethal (a truly reasonable possibility). If we assume most genes are essential for life, the likely outcome of such mutations would be death for those individuals who acquired the altered genes. The natural selection process immediately and unapologetically purges them. On the surface, the seeming coldness of this verdict seems fatalistic and final—at least from the perspective of those individuals carrying the compromised genes. But this is not the end of the story. It turns out that biological systems are primarily geared for *ultimate* physical/biological survival. Not for the short term or even for a particular individual, but for the long term and the population as a whole. And to the Random Designer, it seems that the long term is accorded the highest value. It provides the opportunity for biology to create something truly spectacular!

So how does this biological survival system work? To understand this concept more fully, visualize a large scenario that also includes those rare cells that experience beneficial mutations (less than 0.00001% of the time in this example). Because the number of positively mutated cells is so incredibly low, they might seem insignificant. However, though exceedingly rare, cells that acquire new positive characteristics are most vital to the overall scheme of things.

In addition, and of great significance to our discussion, *beneficial mutations need only happen once* within a cell for that change to become a permanent part of the cell's genetic makeup. Once it is there, it is typically there for good.

These biological phenomena of mutation and positive selection occur continuously in virtually all life. And they are very easy to document. For example, suppose 1,000,000,000 (1 billion) bacteria are grown in a test tube culture. If an antibiotic is then added to the culture, the antibiotic will probably kill more than 99.999999% of the bacteria. On the surface, this seems like a completely lethal effect, but in reality it is not. If the drug destroys 99.999999% of the bacteria, this means that 0.000001% of the original population possesses the genetic capability to survive. Therefore, simple mathematics dictates that there would actually be 1,000 survivors. These surviving bacteria, reproducing every fifteen minutes under optimal conditions, would, in just a few hours, create a whole new population (billions) of antibiotic resistant bacteria. (Figure 9.1)

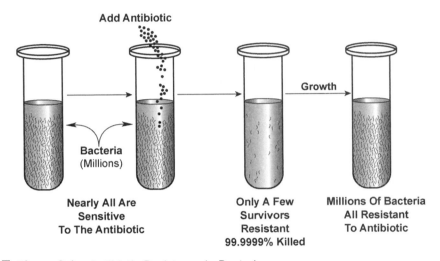

Figure 9.1   Antibiotic Resistance in Bacteria

Scientists observe scenarios such as these in multitudes of real biological populations, although the time periods required for more complex organisms are generally much longer. Under the "right" conditions, cells and organisms that acquire *positive* mutations are able to survive, and even thrive, in their modified form.

One more point is most pertinent to this discussion. As explained in the previous example, positive survival traits are faithfully transmitted to all of the organism's descendants. In this way, the selected organisms and their modified genetic constitution now comprise a brand new genetic foundation. Upon this base, additional positive changes in the DNA slowly accumulate to establish yet another new biological foundation.

The overall net effect is a self-propagating and sequentially assembling synthesis system built into the very framework of biological existence, creating an endless cycle of positive growth and development within each living creation. With the passage of long periods of time and many generations, this stepwise accumulation of positive changes gradually produces an infinite number of biological possibilities. New structure, new functions, new organization, and even the creation of capabilities beyond our current comprehension become legitimately conceivable within the context of living things.

In summary, most mutations in living organisms are harmful. The consequence is that living things routinely experience millions upon millions of failures. Yet amid a multitude of failures, only one success is needed to propel life forward in a beneficial way. Thus, random design conducts one worldwide and perpetual optimization experiment within every living creature and each of its cells. This experiment relentlessly searches for the best biological solutions and designs—those optimally suited for the prevailing conditions. In this way, life continually adapts to changing conditions and progresses toward the highest possible levels of physical existence.

This grand platform of mutation and selection appears to be the best and perhaps the only workable solution for the vast challenges to biological development. It effectively provides the diversification potential to process countless possibilities (mutations), yet is still able to arrive at meaningful and productive conclusions. It is both the mechanism and the miracle that drives all of biology toward its ultimate destinations.

The Dynamics of Mutation and Change— Compromise

The extraordinary value of the random design paradigm is that it creates many wonderful possibilities for life. And its development potential is clearly evidenced by the results—extraordinary biological diversity. In addition, the versatility of the process is equally impressive. In fact, both negative *and* positive consequences can spring from a *single* mutational event.

Human beings possess two copies of each gene—one from the mother and one from the father. Individuals with two copies of the normal hemoglobin gene are fully susceptible to malaria. On the other hand, those who acquire two copies of the sickle-cell gene are fully susceptible to the lethal effects of sickle-cell anemia. However, individuals who possess one copy of each gene can live reasonably normal lives. In addition, they are more resistant to the disease malaria. So in this case, biology has embarked upon a precarious balancing act—attempting to reconcile the selective pressures of an infectious disease with the body's oxygen needs. To understand the reality and success of this scenario, consider that in human populations around the globe, the highest number of individuals possessing the "inferior" sickle-cell gene is routinely observed in tropical areas where malaria occurs most frequently.

This biological response is clearly a compromise, and compromise is another word that sometimes carries a negative connotation. However, for many individuals, especially those who prove resistant to malaria and are living in tropical locales, *compromise has a positive outcome.*

This grand platform of mutation and selection appears to be the best and perhaps the only workable solution to the vast challenges to biological development. It is both the mechanism and the miracle that drives all of biology toward its ultimate destinations.

Thus, as a general premise, when biological/physical survival is at stake, survival uniformly receives the highest priority. But when confronted with the most challenging conditions, biology does not always engage in simple yes/no decisions. It sometimes responds in a graded fashion. In this way, life can innately evaluate many unique situations, finding the most comprehensive and excellent solutions to each new challenge.

These observations elicit questions regarding how such fine-tuned decision-making processes actually occur within the limited submicroscopic confines of tiny living cells. Indeed, integrating the many individual biological components into a clear and unambiguous understanding of life is a challenge. Scientists have worked for many years to reach the current level of comprehension and insight, and there is still much to learn. Nevertheless, biologists do understand that mutation/selection processes work. They utilize the opposite extremes of change and stasis, adaptation and death, as well as randomness and order to accomplish one of the most incredible balancing acts imaginable—creating, preserving, and extending life.

A Beautiful Balancing Act

Diversity and Preservation Come to Terms

Balance, balance, balance! When it comes to creating genetic diversity and improved versions of living organisms, an extremely delicate and fragile equilibrium exists between life and death. On one hand, sufficient mutational potential must be built into the cell's genetics to allow all living organisms to appropriately change and adapt to varying environmental conditions. At the same time, the most essential genes coding for key structures and functions in living organisms must be guarded and conserved with a high degree of fidelity. Very few mistakes or errors in these foundational cellular genes are tolerated.

To cite a previous example, our cells now resemble a finely tuned Swiss watch—except for one important detail: Once a Swiss watch is completely assembled, there are no further adjustments. It is considered a perfect instrument with no need for additional change. In contrast, biology is in a continual state of flux, expanding the cell's genes through gene duplication, controlled mutation, and selection. The stakes for all life in this matter are extremely high. Excessively high mutation rates would break down the essential fabric and core foundations of living things, while mutation rates that are too low would inhibit adaptation and developmental potential. This ongoing tension between preserving the best of the present while concurrently allowing for future growth and development is the cornerstone of all life on our planet.

Preservation Is the Highest Priority!

Living cells seem to recognize that a strong preservation principle is needed. Indeed, the cell's highest priority is guarding the treasured gene combinations that are most essential for life. Living cells today provide clear examples of this fact: Virtually all life utilizes a common core of functional genes. This core genetic information is shared by many diverse species such as bacteria, fruit flies, plants, and humans. As expected, the protein products of these genes play key survival roles for the organisms, roles such as utilization of the energy molecule glucose, and protection and maintenance of the genetic information itself—characteristics shared by all living cells. Therefore, it comes as no surprise that when the chemical base sequences of these genes are compared, only slight variations are observed, even across widely divergent species. These observations lead scientists to conclude that the value of these common genes is so high that they have been rigorously preserved for eons through multiple generations and random mutation/selection regimens.

But not all genes are conserved in this fashion. Many non-core genes are also present in living organisms, and, as expected, these genes display much wider variation. Frequently, they are completely unique to a particular organism.

The supreme value of the preservation principle is also supported by another interesting and remarkable observation: *The cell corrects its own mistakes/mutations as it reproduces itself.* The biological implications arising from this fact are enormous, but to address the full significance of this incredible feature we need a basic understanding of cell reproduction.

Reproduction of Living Cells

Before any living cell divides or reproduces, it must first make a duplicate copy of its DNA. This is no small task: Remember, there are over six billion bases in the chromosomes of each cell. Nevertheless, the cell is easily up to the challenge, completing the entire process in a mere hour or so. Once the DNA is copied, the cell divides, equally distributing the two DNA molecules (chromosomes) to the two new daughter cells. (Figure 10.1)

Thanks to this chromosome segregation, each daughter cell acquires a full complement of the information (genes) encoded in the DNA sequences. As discussed earlier, these genes direct production

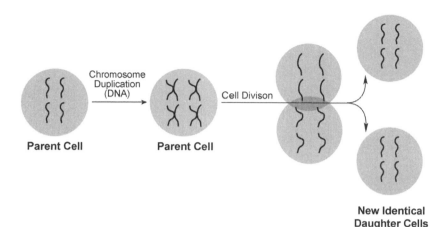

Figure 10.1   Duplication of Chromosomes

of the essential life-giving cellular proteins. Hence, faithful DNA duplication or replication is fundamental, universal, and crucial to all living cells and organisms. Without a reliable replication scheme, genes would be grossly miscopied and these altered cells would certainly die.

A specialized replicator protein, called DNA polymerase, carries out the DNA copying. Existing DNA acts as a template, or blueprint, from which a new and identical DNA strand is constructed. The actual replication operation is truly spectacular: Up to fifty new chemical bases are stitched together each second as the new DNA chain forms. In addition, the precision of the operation is mind-boggling: Errors are rare.

To illustrate the magnitude of this task, suppose you had a string of fifty styrofoam balls in a preset sequence of four different colors. Now, provided you have access to an ample supply of colored balls, you can attempt to duplicate the sequence of colored balls onto a new string. The multiple steps you would go through would involve: first, recognizing the appropriately colored ball; second, picking up the ball; third, inserting the string through the ball; and fourth, sliding it into position on the string. Even with our visual abilities, advanced intellectual processing powers, and manual dexterity, I doubt that more than one ball could be assembled per second. The demands are just too great. But as difficult as this feat is for us, it is relatively easy for the submicroscopic DNA polymerase. It not only performs the task, but does it exceedingly well. Figure 10.2 illustrates this process.

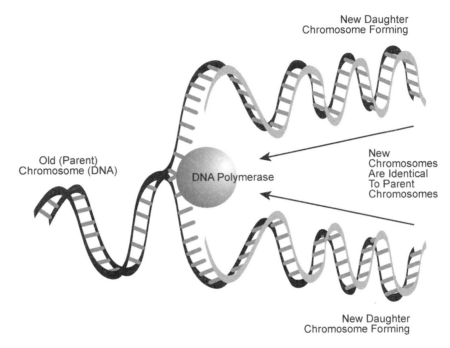

Figure 10.2   DNA Replication

Scientists postulate that the first DNA polymerase of early living cells on earth was simple and rudimentary. Consequently, this DNA polymerase was probably prone to high error rates and failed to copy the template DNA with a high degree of precision. In contrast, modern DNA polymerase enzymes make relatively few errors. So what is the difference? The reason for the improvement is that DNA polymerase enzymes observed in today's cells possess an important add-on feature that enables a second function—the ability to edit its work. This self-editing function means that the new DNA is automatically corrected when mutations occur. In this manner, new DNA is reproduced quickly and accurately with markedly reduced errors.

The fact that even the DNA polymerase enzymes of simple bacteria have this self-editing function suggests that the fidelity of DNA replication was accorded a high priority even in simple cells of an early earth. And as cells gradually become more complex, keeping mistakes to a minimum during DNA replication becomes even more critical for survival. Without it, random error rates and harmful mutations would be far too high to support and maintain life. Yet, even though this self-editing feature is a useful characteristic and makes DNA replication more accurate, the process is still not quite perfect. For every million or so chemical bases that it copies, the enzyme occasionally goofs and accidentally incorporates an incorrect chemical base into the new DNA strand. From our previous discussion, you will recognize this change as a mutation. *Therefore, in reality, the only mutations observed in real life are the ones that escape this editing function!*

So from a biological perspective, even though mutations still occur, a low mutation rate of one in a million or so appears to be acceptable. It allows for some variability while retaining the high priority to preserve the established order of genes within a cell.

Preservation Counterpoint— More Mutation Please!

The DNA replication system I have described seems to work well for simple organisms like bacteria. But for more complex organisms such as plants, animals, and humans, there arises an unexpected problem. Under the restrictive/low mutation rate imposed by the self-editing function of the DNA polymerase, genetic modifications apparently do not occur fast enough to meet these higher organisms' more sophisticated adaptation needs.

But how can this be? If mutations are usually harmful, the best course would seem to be keeping mutations at an absolute minimum or eliminating them altogether. But surprisingly, low mutation rates are not always best. In fact, not only is mutation a tolerable event, some mutation (change) is actually desirable. It creates variation, and variation is the fuel for progress in biology.

Therefore, the low mutation rate associated with the self-correcting characteristic of the DNA polymerase creates a biological bottleneck. Complicated systems of more highly developed cells and organisms require a faster rate of change in order to successfully adapt.

Controlled Random Variation

In response to this genetic bottleneck, higher organisms have developed several spectacular ways to significantly increase genetic variation within their cells. This accelerated variation must retain the essential elements of randomness in order to produce the maximum number of possibilities. However, it must also operate within carefully controlled parameters in order to maintain established cell order.

It seems like another paradox. Whoever heard of such a thing—controlled random variation! But as unlikely as it may seem, it is commonplace in living organisms. One of the easiest ways for cells to accomplish controlled random variations is to utilize existing genes. Genes can be duplicated, exchanged, or shared between different individuals. In this way, individuals acquire *variant forms* of established genes rather than always relying upon random variations to create *new genes* themselves. The process is comparable to a common practice among college roommates. Rather than individually buying ten separate outfits, the students mix and match clothes to produce a greater number of unique combinations. A similar tactic in biology allows some degree of continued variation, but restricts most of the variation to changes within established genes—a type of controlled variation. The best-understood system of exchanging or sharing genes occurs during the process known as sexual reproduction. And this remarkable dimension of sexual reproduction elevates life to a new state of biological existence.

The Benefits of Sex

In the current context, the primary long-term benefit of sexual reproduction is its ability to enhance genetic diversity by mixing and matching existing genes. It carefully blends the essential elements of balance and preservation into a system that moves biology forward in more systematic and organized ways.

Genetic variation reaches a new level of sophistication in sexually reproducing organisms. Individual random mutations now become smaller subplots to much larger schemes for generating genetic diversity.

The most well-known and best-understood mechanism occurs during the development of sperm cells in males and egg cells in females. During the process of generating these sex cells, chromosomes mix and match in totally random ways. The result is a mathematically mind-dazzling array of different gene combinations. For example, from just one set of human parents, the probability of two siblings (other than identical twins) being exactly alike is easily less than one in a trillion. (That is the number one with twelve trailing zeros.) This number is more than 150 times greater than the earth's current human population. Diversity indeed! Many a sibling will take considerable consolation in this fact: Even though a brother or sister may appear similar in many ways, they can be assured that at the most fundamental level they really are different.

Sexual reproduction thus appears to be the pinnacle of biological development as it relates to the creation of stable but moldable genetic diversity. It preserves the essential gene sets necessary for life, yet still offers open-ended possibilities for improvement by mixing and matching existing gene variants. These diversity-inducing mechanisms are possible because each cell of the body possesses *two functional copies of each gene* instead of just one. The father's sperm provides one gene copy while the mother's egg provides the other.

An additional benefit of having two copies of each gene is that if a *harmful* random mutation occurs within one copy of a gene, it does not necessarily produce harmful effects on the entire cell or organism. A fully functional backup copy within the cell can usually maintain the gene's essential activity and allow cells to survive.

Some cancers provide a vivid example of this effect. Scientists have identified a dynamic cellular gene called p53 that appears to play a central role in maintaining normal cell division and preventing development of many cancers. Cells that possess one defective/mutated p53 gene generally still behave normally because of the backup copy. However, the presence of two defective copies of the p53 gene places the cell at high risk to become cancerous.[1-3] Figure 10.3 illustrates this principle.

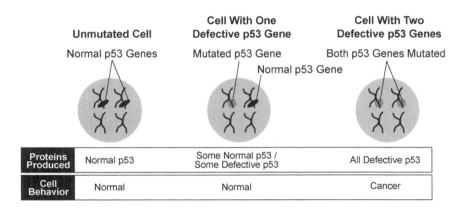

Figure 10.3   Tumor Suppressor p53 Gene and Cancer

As we have seen so many times, the primary directive of biology is to survive, and living organisms utilize extraordinary means to accomplish this mission. Every life form from the very beginning of time has developed in strict obedience to the fundamental rules of nature dictated by the Random Designer. Error, mutation, variation, and selection are all part of these rules around which life revolves. Violations are simply not tolerated, and violators are either disregarded or ruthlessly eliminated.

When all components of life are carefully studied and assembled into a coherent package, the confusing and extraordinary dynamics begin to crystallize into sharp focus. Contrary to popular contemporary consensus, mutation and change are not the antithesis of life. They are the very essence of a vibrant, pulsing, and surging life. Natural selection is not at odds with the Random Designer. It is a part of His process and plan. *Some people say that evolution proves there is no Creator. On the contrary, evolution tells us how remarkably creative God really is!*

Evolution and natural selection function together, to bring immense beauty and order out of disorder, by testing nearly every imaginable variation. They unemotionally and methodically leave the unworkable behind and steadfastly move onward and forward. The result is an endless process of trial and error that automatically searches for solutions and paths leading to newer and higher levels of existence! This magnificent and greatly under-appreciated regimen of discovery has functioned from the beginning of time on our planet with astounding results—us!

The search for life's best continues to this very day. And it is fueled by the rules of randomness.

Evolution

A Brief Chronology of Life on Earth

11

The processes of mutation and natural selection, along with even more advanced mechanisms for creating genetic diversity, establish a powerful platform that propels living organisms forward. One early and very significant product of this platform was the creation of the first simple multicellular organisms. Evolving over hundreds of millions of years, these organisms gradually led to more highly developed species such as plants, fish, amphibians, reptiles, birds, and mammals. The scientific record not only substantiates the existence of these creatures, but also primarily validates their persistent progression over time.

Although the evidence for evolution arises from various fields of science that generally corroborate well, the clearest visual support for evolution comes from the images of living beings embedded within the rocks of the earth. These images are called fossils.

Although no one can put an absolute definitive date to it, the fossil trail of life apparently began about 3.8 billion years ago and has continued all the way to the present. Knowing that rock layers form sequentially over long periods of time, geologists use radioisotope dating techniques and several other corroborating methods to approximate the actual age of rocks. These techniques are quite easy to understand, and although their accuracy is not perfect, they still provide close estimations of when a rock and its contents came into being.

How does this rock record lead to the understanding that living things existed millions or even billions of years ago?

Perhaps the easiest way to explain this concept is with an analogy. At my house we receive two daily newspapers—one local and one international.

Each day the papers are spread over the dining room table as different family members read their favorite sections. At the end of the day the newspapers are gathered, carefully folded, and stacked on the pantry floor. Over days and weeks, the newspaper stack steadily grows higher. Of course, the papers are intermittently transferred to the recycling bin in the garage, but suppose we let the stack accumulate indefinitely. Over a long period of time, the stack would form a layered "clock," depicting a linear and historical catalogue of events captured in the words and pictures of the newspapers.

In the same way, scientists are able to map out a chronology, or sequence of events, from the fossils they find embedded within rock layers. For example, an image of a fish found in a rock layer formed 150 million years ago would logically indicate the fish must also be 150 million years old.

Some people, for a variety of reasons, regard these scientific age measurements with skepticism. Even in the face of overwhelming evidence telling us that the earth is very old and that life has existed on our planet for a long time, these people believe the science is suspect. To them, such long time periods are unfathomable and therefore just too difficult to believe.

Certainly, hundreds of millions of years is a very long time, but hopefully you are beginning to see that just because something is hard to conceive does not mean it is untrue. The truth is that the scientific time measurement tools have been rigorously tested and verified in many independent ways. Because of this fact, and to eliminate any perceived ambiguity regarding this topic, two pointed statements must be made. First of all, fossils are real! Anyone with functioning eyesight can see them. Second, fossils are extremely old. Therefore, although the scientific data does not support a literal Biblical view of an 8,000 to 12,000-year-old earth, the information derived from these tools must be considered valid. There is no rational basis for continued denial.

Does this mean scientists are in wholehearted agreement on every issue related to age measurements or evolution? Of course not! Engaged scientists often disagree. However, these disagreements generally relate to specific interpretations of the fossil record, including precise age determinations, or how and why living things changed from one form to another during millions of years of early earth history. Some people scoff at the scientific process because by its nature, it allows and even encourages second-guessing. They say that if scientists can be wrong about one thing, then we cannot confidently believe anything they tell us. But these people fail to realize that this is the beauty of science: Our understanding of the physical world can be changed by just one good experiment. Dynamic and spirited debate is a vital and healthy part of the overall process.

Therefore, it seems to me that rather than ridiculing scientists, the volunteered vulnerability of science should breed confidence in the overall validity of conclusions. There is virtually complete scientific consensus on the general principles of evolution and that life has existed on our planet for hundreds of millions of years.

This chapter does not provide a detailed description of fossils, evolutionary pathways, or evidence supporting these pathways. Frankly, unanswered questions regarding the exact routes and time frames of evolution abound. Responding to every minute criticism and question regarding the process could easily become a full-time endeavor a scenario I intend to *vigorously avoid*! However, with the caveat that much of our understanding is continually being fine-tuned, it does seem important to provide an overview of the scientific thinking in this area. This general overview, depicted in Figure 11.1, is easily found in any introductory textbook on the topic and provides a snapshot visual image of the earth's truly astonishing records of life.[1]

First Signs

The earliest signs of life on our planet come from indirect data that is still somewhat tentative. This knowledge is based on clues left by organisms that were able to carry out the process of photosynthesis. Recalling from chapter five, the central role of carbon in all living things, the scenario presents itself as follows: When photosynthesis occurs, the living cell takes carbon dioxide from the air and simultaneously releases oxygen. During photosynthesis, carbon atoms

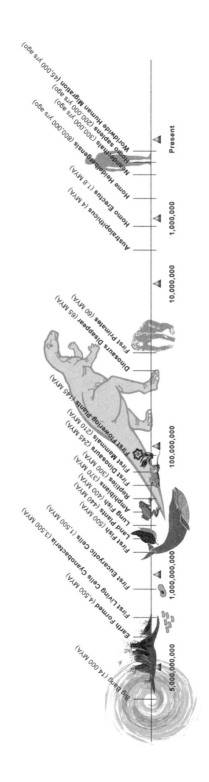

Figure 11.1 Earth Life History Timeline

from the absorbed carbon dioxide are incorporated into the cell's organic molecules—proteins, sugars, nucleic acids, and fats.

Of particular importance is the fact that naturally occurring carbon exists in two different forms called isotopes. Scientists designate these two isotopes carbon 12 and carbon 13. One unusual feature of photosynthesis is that it prefers to accumulate the carbon 12 isotope in the cells at a higher rate than the carbon 13 isotope. Consequently, rock layers formed around photosynthetic organisms would naturally contain higher levels of the carbon 12 isotope. Some of the oldest known rocks on earth are found in Greenland and have been dated at about 3.85 billion years old. Although still tentative, the fact that these rocks are enriched in the carbon 12 isotope suggests that primitive photosynthetic life may have been present even at this very early stage of the earth's history.[2] Consistent with this finding, some of the earliest fossil remains are of primitive photosynthetic bacteria. These organisms are known as Cyanobacteria.

The Procaryotes—Cyanobacteria

The Cyanobacteria belong to a large group of simple organisms called procaryotes. Most bacteria are included in this group. The presence of Cyanobacteria appears to reliably date back about 3.5 billion years. Scientists suspect that initially these organisms were able to grow in the absence of oxygen (anaerobic) and proliferated in large dense mineralized marine mats called stromatolites. The biochemistry of these organisms is especially interesting. Scientists believe the earliest living cells may have utilized inorganic (non-carbon) compounds such as hydrogen sulfide as one of their early energy sources, a characteristic actually observed in some contemporary species of Cyanobacteria. This observation suggests that in addition to photosynthesis, these organisms could also capture energy, albeit very inefficiently, from inorganic compounds. Early life forms may have used this ancillary energy source until they developed more efficient oxygen or photosynthetic mechanisms to capture energy.

Amazingly, for nearly 2 billion years it appears the Cyanobacteria, along with a few other simple microorganisms called Archaebacteria, were virtually alone on the planet. But conditions were certainly not static during this time. Remember that one of the products of photosynthesis is molecular oxygen. Hence, this expansive 2-billion-year stretch of time was an important incubation period. As the gradual release and accumulation of oxygen generated a global atmosphere, the earth and conditions on its surface began changing in astonishing ways. And once oxygen levels reached a critical threshold, the world and the life living in it would never be the same.

Oxygen

One of the most significant consequences of oxygen buildup was probably related to its effect on the earth's environment, particularly in the oxygenation of the seas and development of an ozone layer/atmosphere. Indeed, scientists believe formation of the ozone layer was critical because ozone filters out ultraviolet rays that are destructive to most life forms. But herein lies another apparent paradox.

While the accumulation of oxygen created a useful barrier to damaging radiation, oxygen also created a significant obstacle to life. Although many organisms today use oxygen (O_2) for their respiration needs, some of oxygen's minor by-products such as superoxide (O_2^-) are actually lethal to most life forms, even at low concentrations. Living cells must be able to eliminate or neutralize these toxic forms of oxygen if they are to survive. Consequently, scientists believe the oxygen obstacle presented a serious survival challenge for life.[2]

Fortunately, molecular oxygen did not instantly appear on earth, but accumulated over billions of years. This long interval apparently gave Cyanobacteria time for random design to solve the superoxide problem. The result was the appearance of a specialized cellular protein called superoxide dysmutase. This protein, which is commonly found in most living organisms, effectively detoxifies the harmful superoxide, allowing living cells such as our own to survive in the presence of high oxygen levels. In addition, the appearance of the superoxide dysmutase and other similar proteins opened spectacular and unexpected new doors of opportunity and possibility for all life. For the first time, instead of being harmed by oxygen, living organisms could now tap into aerobic (oxygen utilizing) respiration, or breathing schemes. These systems allowed living organisms to capture the energy of organic compounds such as glucose much more efficiently.

In fact, scientists today understand that (aerobic) oxygen respiration is a true boon to life. Aerobic (oxygen utilizing) respiration, found in all air-breathing organisms, is able to capture energy from glucose (recall coupled chemical reactions from chapter three) at levels nearly twenty times more efficient than simple anaerobic (no oxygen) respiration. All things considered, it seems that high oxygen levels were pivotal for life to progress. Indeed, the fact that all advanced life forms today use oxygen attests to its significant value for capturing and utilizing energy.

Eucaryotes

Most living cells today are neatly categorized into one of two major groups. The first group, already discussed, is called *procaryotes,* and includes most bacteria, including the Cyanobacteria. The second group of more highly developed cells is called *eucaryotes,* meaning true nucleus. Indeed, the most prominent feature distinguishing procaryotes from eucaryotes is that procaryotes lack a well-defined nucleus—the internal cell structure that houses the chromosomes. In contrast, all eucaryotic cells, including those of plants, animals, and even humans, have well-defined nuclear structures. Many striking similarities exist in the genetics and biochemistry of these two cell groups, implying a common ancestry, but there are also unmistakable differences. Overall, the eucaryotes are more complex and superior in many ways.

Current scientific evidence suggests the evolutionary move from simple Cyanobacteria (procaryote) to the creation of true eucaryotic cells occurred about 1.5 billion years ago. In other words, bacteria were the only inhabitants of earth for about 2 billion years.

Eucaryotes may have been direct ancestors of procaryotes, or they may have descended from a separate distinct line of living cells. The scientific evidence, while favoring the first alternative, is not totally conclusive. Nonetheless, the appearance of eucaryotic cells seems to have marked yet another significant beginning for biological development. Today we see that virtually all advanced life forms are eucaryotic in nature. Representative classes of eucaryotic life include plants, fish, amphibians, reptiles, and mammals.

Plants

The earliest marine plants (photosynthetic algae) were evidently among the first eucaryotic cells. Scientists suspect marine plant life played a vital ecological role for the development of later creatures, such as fish and amphibians. However, scientific evidence also indicates that the more rugged land plant fossils did not appear until later—about 440 million years ago. The transition of life from sea to land was not a sudden event: It appears to have occurred over a very long time—perhaps up to a billion years. But even among plants, the random design, mutation/selection process appears to have functioned successfully, resulting in diverse genetic populations of plant species that have come and gone over millions of years. Major biological adaptations, such as the creation of flowering plants, are more recent in plant evolution, showing up in the fossil record around 145 million years ago. Continued plant evolution and diversification have progressed even to modern times.

While plants do not possess a direct evolutionary connection to animal life or human beings, they are nonetheless vitally important. Plants have played an essential ancillary role to the continuance of all life. In fact, the crucial contribution of plants for life on earth is difficult to overstate. Already at a very early stage in the history of life on earth, a system of interdependent relationships was being forged among quite different and unique living things. For example, flowering plants and pollinating insects are intricately tied together in a web of mutual survival. Similarly, by effectively tapping the energy reservoir of the sun, plants provide a short-term solution to the inevitable destructive tendencies associated with the

Second Law of Thermodynamics: Plants give an abundance of food, oxygen, cover, and other materials needed by various living species. Ultimately, they provide the energy and resources needed to make all other higher forms of life on earth possible.

Fish

The earliest fish fossils are around 500 million years old. Biologists find these organisms particularly interesting because they were among the first to possess a nerve cord (nervous system) and vertebrae (backbone). During the first 100 million years after this group's appearance, significant evolutionary changes are evident in the fossil record. One group of fish even developed an incredibly novel and useful structure—air-breathing lungs. As bizarre as it may seem, these lungs allowed this group of fish to actually survive in water *or* on land. This movement of life out of the water is considered a significant milestone for life on earth, leading to the development of land life. In addition, fossil evidence demonstrates that some of these fish actually possessed fin bone structure with an appearance more like limbs (feet). Evolutionary scholars believe amphibians derived from this or a similar group of early fish.

Amphibians

The earliest amphibian fossils are found in rocks dated around 370 million years ago. By this time, evidence shows some of these organisms had developed significant modifications in their anatomy (legs, feet, shoulders, necks, jaws, and skulls). Presumably, these changes helped them adapt much better to life on land. Thus, amphibians were probably the first animal to successfully and routinely move from water to land. Evolutionary scientists contend that a very early line of amphibians ultimately led to modern amphibians such as the frogs and toads recognized today. Another interesting and distinct line of early amphibians was apparently the precursor to a group of animals called anthracosaurs. These animals are significant because they took on a remarkable reptilian appearance.

Reptiles

The first fossilized reptiles appear in the rock record about 300 million years ago. Generally speaking, reptiles are usually envisioned as gigantic dinosaurs and fierce crocodiles. However, scientific evidence suggests the first reptiles were actually quite small—perhaps only a few inches long. The fossil record also suggests that reptiles were very successful as a group, thriving on land and developing tremendous diversity over millions of years. One group of reptiles (the theropods) is particularly noteworthy. Theropods appear to be linked to dinosaurs and also birds.

The first dinosaurs (just one unique group of reptiles) are evident in the fossil record beginning around 245 million years ago. As human beings, we seem to have a universal fascination with these ancient creatures: They were both magnificent and intimidating. Adding to this fascination, the movie industry, plus many elementary school textbooks and natural history museums, have extended the popularity of these creatures. Dinosaurs appear to have dominated life on land for over 100 million years, until their mass extinction around 65 million years ago.

Mammals

The first mammal fossils appear in rocks that are approximately 210 million years old. Scientists believe that they evolved from a select reptilian group called Cynodonts. While significant differences exist between reptiles and mammals today, these groups also have remarkable similarities. Most contemporary mammals are quite small—less than a couple of pounds. In fact, larger mammals are the exception to the rule. One significant difference between mammals and all other life is that mammals possess larger and more highly developed brains than earlier species. As expected, the acquisition of a more sophisticated brain and nervous system provided mammals with enhanced sensory and motor (movement) capabilities, allowing them to perceive and adapt more readily to changing conditions.

Although the first mammals were apparently present more than 200 million years ago, they did not initially achieve the levels of success seen with the reptiles in terms of overall numbers or land dominance. However, following the sudden and mysterious extinction of the dinosaurs approximately 65 million years ago, mammals experienced tremendous expansion both in numbers and diversification.[3] Some find it intriguing that the disappearance of the dinosaurs at this point in the earth's history closely corresponds with the approximate date the first primates appeared. Following this well-documented and dramatic disappearing act, the large-brained primates with their superior mental development potential could develop more freely, unimpeded by the strong competitive pressures imposed by the dinosaurs.

Today, mammals comprise two major groups—the marsupials (kangaroos and opossums) and the placentals (all other mammals, including humans).

Primates

Primates are a much larger and diverse group of mammals to which humans belong. Although humans are primates, not all primates are humans. Current scientific evidence suggests there were originally two families of primates—the small-brain prosimians and the larger-brain anthropoids, who appeared about 60 million years ago. The anthropoid group breaks down into two categories. The first category includes the monkeys; the second category comprises the hominoids, including apes, gibbons, and humans. In addition to fossil evidence, which indicates close relatedness, current genetic evidence also reveals over 98% correspondence between the genes of chimpanzees (apes) and humans. It is significant to note, however, that even though chimpanzees and humans apparently share many of their genes, and even appear to derive from an approximately 6-million-year-old common hominoid ancestor, it is not currently believed that humans evolved from chimpanzees. Humans appear to have developed from a separate and distinct hominid lineage.[4,5]

The fossil record indicates that many hominid species have existed on earth, including a large group called Australopithicus, which first appeared in fossils dated about 4 million years ago. An even more advanced group of hominids called Homo (human like) appear in fossils dated around 2 million years ago. Several sub-groups of Homo (perhaps individual species?) have also been discovered from fossil remains at many sites around the world. While the first Homo species had limited brain size and likely possessed corresponding limited intellectual capabilities, later species show clear evidence of a larger brain. In fact, Neanderthal and Cro-Magnon fossils, some dated as recently as 30,000 to 100,000 years ago, suggest that these relatively advanced creatures had a physical structure and brain size closely comparable to modern humans.

Humans

So where does this discussion of primates and hominids finally lead in regard to human beings? When it comes to making clear and unequivocal distinctions between creatures which obviously differ in outward appearance yet bear striking similarity in their underlying genetics to modern humans, we are left with the unmistakable picture that we are much more similar than different, and that our heritage is closely intertwined.

This idea leads to the fundamental question of what truly set modern humans apart from these pre-humans. Frankly, it is a difficult question. Perhaps the answer is something very distinctive and evident, such as language, or maybe something more subtle and intriguing is involved. Realistically, the answer is not completely clear. But while scientists disagree on the explicit details of human development, there is a fairly uniform consensus that anatomically modern Homo sapiens (modern man) developed as an extraordinary branch from a special and unique population of Africans sometime between 100,000 and 200,000 years ago. Then, around 45,000 years ago, a line of these talented and versatile modern humans radiated out to populate and subdue the rest of the world.

And the Random Designer observed all He had created on earth, and He saw that it was very good.

Random Design and Faith

Searching for Purpose and Meaning in a Randomness-Driven World

In the preceding chapters of section I, some basic scientific and biological concepts were introduced. As you can plainly see, the origin and development of life on our planet are indeed complex propositions. The laws of physics and chemistry have acted in unexpected and seemingly miraculous ways to create something scientists are just beginning to comprehend—human life.

I have suggested that science has great authority to describe the physical world around us, but that it is not so effective when dealing with some of life's most important considerations—such as relationships, meaning, and purpose. Nevertheless, I believe science *can* provide useful insights into the magnificent design that is apparent in the final product—us.

Certainly, no one would disagree that all forms of life, from simple to more advanced, show clear evidence of design. Many people believe this design element is evidence in and of itself for the existence of a Designer. But as we have seen in preceding chapters, the natural laws of physics and chemistry also appear to be able to create—all on their own. And this information leads to a central question.

Does the understanding that life arose as a result of natural law eliminate the need or possibility of a Designer?

Some individuals believe this is indeed the case. However, such a conclusion does not fully respond to the question, but simply pushes it back to a more fundamental level. For if one concludes that natural causes are responsible for the creation of life, it begs the question of who created the natural laws: Who energized all of creation in the first place? And even if the natural laws somehow came into existence by themselves, how did they possess just the right characteristics to accomplish the incredible biosynthetic feats so clearly observed in life today? As I see it, the essence of the matter boils down to a simple statement: *Science cannot prove or disprove God's existence. Belief in a Master Designer is ultimately an individual decision. It is a matter of faith.*

As outlined in chapter two, contemporary culture often gives the impression that we have only two options—evolution (no designer and no purpose) or creationism (a designer with a purpose).

Hopefully by now you understand that these two options are not the only ones. The scientific underpinnings of mutation and selection, along with the powerful synthesis platform these processes provide for creating life, suggest a Creator who is a Random Designer. The Designer simply established these random processes as the best tools to accomplish His purposes.

If there really is a Designer (God) behind all of creation, it would suggest the possibility and potential for a higher purpose and meaning to our existence. If for no other reason than this, I believe that we owe it to ourselves to honestly consider the possibilities.

Realistically, it is difficult to deny the compelling scientific observations and evidences that continually accumulate. In this book, we have already considered the following: The Second Law of Thermodynamics, the formation of chemical elements, the age of the earth, energy capture and utilization, coupled chemical reactions that provide synthesis capabilities in biology, information transfer, communication mechanisms, mutation and selection, very simple life forms giving way to progressively higher and higher life forms over vast periods of time, a clearly documented fossil record of many of these events, and finally, less developed human-like beings inhabiting our planet between 30,000 and 2 million years ago.

And here we stand as complex, intelligent, and conscious creatures contemplating our past and wondering about design and purpose. Incredible!

Some people, on religious grounds, choose to aggressively ignore or deny many scientific concepts and principles, especially in the domain of evolution. This is not a new or surprising development. People have responded in similar fashion to many of science's most dramatic discoveries. For example, in the early 1500s Copernicus and Galileo proposed that planets revolved around the sun and that earth was not the center of the universe. This concept, considered common knowledge today, was viewed as religious heresy at the time because it implied that mankind might actually be able to determine how the world worked. Imagine that!

The problem, as I see it, is that we tend to squeeze God into small rigid boxes of our own making to keep Him conceptually consistent with our traditional religious beliefs. Unfortunately, this approach to religious faith is fraught with liability because it prevents God from truly being God—a creator capable of using *any means* He chooses for His creation.

Whenever theological doctrine is rigidly linked to observed physical phenomena, religious faith itself teeters in the balance. As scientific understanding of the world changes and relentlessly marches forward, a religious faith that is unchangeable is doomed. Furthermore, the intellectual credibility of those who refuse to let God out of the box will be weakened, and their authority to speak on other important social issues will be significantly compromised.

It appears that in a very real sense God truly is a Random Designer. But this understanding need not be a problem for our faith. Quite the contrary! While some people may find the Random Designer concept difficult to fully accept, the truth is that the scientific facts are also God's facts. They really are friendly! We simply have not grasped the magnitude of the possibilities before now. Therefore, mankind's new challenge is to absorb this scientific understanding and integrate it into a meaningful faith and worldview.

Section II of *Random Designer* addresses this issue. The story is incomplete, but I believe it is much more significant and profound than generally recognized. I also believe that courageous honesty is necessary as we try and fit the pieces together. Undoubtedly, many difficult questions will arise. This has certainly been the case for me. But God is not put off by our wondering and our questioning. I believe He even welcomes our curiosity!

Quite possibly, when all is said and done the complete details of His creative mechanisms will never be totally understood. But this in no way diminishes the beauty, magnificence, and powerful significance of His creation or the ultimate results of His extraordinary creative processes. Purpose can still prevail!

I believe we have spent far too much time debating how we were physically created. It is now time to fully focus our thoughts and energies toward discovering *why* we were created. In this crucial endeavor, no one person is greater than another. We are all fellow travelers. And in a very real sense, both biologically and spiritually, we are all brothers.

In this second section, I depart somewhat from the comfortable and secure quarters of science to which I am accustomed, and foray into the less precise and predictable domains of faith and human experience. Positions in these areas are much more difficult to define and defend, but I am convinced they are of utmost importance to discuss. In fact, I have come to believe that our personal faith and interpersonal human experiences may be far and away the most meaningful components of our existence.

Please take careful note that, like many of you, I have numerous questions and only tentative answers. So, in a sense, section II is a personal progress report—the best efforts of one broadly trained scientist attempting to integrate scientific understanding and his life experiences into a coherent foundation of faith. Since the thoughts expressed here are my personal reflections and arise from my own experiences, they should not be afforded the same gravity or weight as the well-established scientific information in the previous chapters.

Concerning matters of religion and faith, there are numerous voices, and many are better qualified to speak than I.

I must also confess that I personally believe God is real. Undoubtedly, this conviction exerts a strong influence on my views, but I do not believe it compromises my credibility to speak on these matters. To the contrary, it seems to me that in the most remarkable and unexpected ways, the decision to acknowledge God's existence is often the first step to a vital relationship with Him.

So, with this information as a background, let's move on to the next section and explore the wonderful possibilities afforded us by the Random Designer.

Who Is Adam?
The Birth of Humanity

12

Genesis, the first book of the Bible, identifies a special individual named Adam as the first human being.[1]

Does the Biblical account actually describe a newly created individual as many people believe? Or does it have a different meaning, defining a focal point in history when human beings acquired new and exceptional distinguishing features that set them apart from their predecessors?

This question elicits extremely strong responses from different individuals depending upon their upbringing, educational background, and religious beliefs. For some, posing such a question borders on religious heresy. On the other hand, the wealth of scientific information points to mankind as the culmination of a cumulative creative process, rather than the product of an instantaneous miraculous event. Therefore, given these diverse opinions, the question seems justified.

Consider also that the Biblical account is not the only creation narrative. There are many religions and each generally has its own traditional version of creation. Not surprisingly, the people espousing a particular viewpoint are usually quite insistent that their account of creation is the only true and valid one. Little room is allowed for differing points of view. Unfortunately, the net effect of taking such adamant positions is that productive dialogue between people of different religious persuasions is automatically precluded. As a consequence, making sense of the bewildering array of religious creation narratives, while at the same time reconciling these accounts with modern scientific understanding, becomes a daunting task.

I find it particularly fascinating that even though various versions of creation may differ markedly in the actual details regarding the beginnings of humankind, they frequently share some commonalities. One noteworthy theme appearing universally in both religious and scientific descriptions of early humanity is that there actually was a definitive beginning point.

Scientists usually describe the beginning of humanity as a single person or a small group of individuals who, through the process of evolution, acquired an advanced biological capability that bestowed upon them a significant survival advantage over other animals and human-like creatures. Religious versions of human creation also point to a single created individual as the originator of the modern human race. They describe this beginning as the point in time at which God supernaturally intervenes in the world, instantaneously and miraculously creating human beings and thus initiating human history. Therefore, apart from differences in the *mechanism* of creation, scientific and religious versions are remarkably quite similar.

In addition to the scientific evidence observed in the fossils, the history of human populations can also be explored by using a variety of other methods, including comparative genetic analysis of DNA.[2-8] These and other scientific methods cast considerable light on the question of human origins, but they are not perfect: They cannot trace human origins back to a single individual. They are only capable of narrowing the search to a small group. Taken together, however, the information arising from these techniques is powerful, because it is both scientifically coherent and consistent with many other scientific and religious viewpoints.

Based upon these scientific findings and combined with the observation that many religious accounts also point to a single original human being, it does not seem unreasonable to surmise that this conclusion is correct. In addition, such an idea fits with an overall understanding of genetics and evolution: Beginning with a single individual, new characteristics and capabilities develop from time to time and these genetic traits are routinely passed on to all offspring.

As discussed earlier, the position actively promoted by some proclaiming the earth and all living things on the earth to be only

8,000 to 12,000 years old is simply scientifically implausible. Strict literal interpretations of Biblical accounts that proclaim the creation of the first man to be from the actual physical dust of the earth are equally dubious. Such literal thinking is perhaps technically and scientifically accurate, since we are all creatures of carbon. However, when it is combined with the section describing the creation of the first woman from a rib of a man, these stories raise serious and understandable questions in the minds of many as to their real purpose.

Are these descriptions actually meant to describe the detailed *mechanisms* of creation, or are they *symbolic* in nature?

If religious accounts of creation are meant to convey an unambiguous message of a definitive beginning point to a most remarkable and momentous event—the creation of humanity as a truly unique race—then it seems to me that instead of being at odds with one another, various religious views might even be complementary. In addition, these views come remarkably close to modern scientific perspectives on this matter.

At this point in the discussion, I can already hear derisive cries directed my way. Those holding more fundamental and conservative religious beliefs will suggest that an explanation of this sort is wholly (not holy) unacceptable. They will claim my intent is to water down God-inspired scriptural content in order to fit a scientific and secular authority paradigm.

Please understand that it is not my intent to evoke such an authority controversy. Believe me I have been there far too many times, with few productive resolutions. In addition, as a person of strong religious belief, I am embarrassed and sad to say that in my experience the most uninformed and closed minds on these subjects are often religious minds. Therefore, little is gained by responding to such charges.

But allow me to provide some balance to the discussion. You see, scientists are people too, and they can also experience a "blinder" mentality on some issues. Therefore, individuals who claim science as the ultimate authority in the world are destined to discover that they are wrong about many things. Likewise, those who insist that rigid, literal scriptural accounts or other religious beliefs are the only ultimate authority will discover they too are severely limited.

The fact of the matter is that the only ultimate authority is God! From this perspective, and since He has authority over all things, perhaps He speaks wisdom and understanding to us from what we learn in science as well as what we learn via the channels of organized religious doctrine. After all, is it reasonable or logical to try to limit Him by arbitrarily closing off certain avenues He might use to illuminate our minds? So with these ideas as background, the time has come for the big question: *What is it, from the perspective of the Creator, that makes humans special—that makes them truly human?*

In many ways, this is the age-old question. Certainly, all would agree that humans truly are exceptional. But the question of what unique features set humans apart from other living creatures on our planet continues to capture our imaginations.

Scientists have proposed a variety of responses to this question. Perhaps one of the most frequent responses is that humans have the capability of self-awareness. But I wonder if we really understand what that concept means.

Perhaps in a very elementary but practical way, it simply means that we can think about what we are thinking about. Think about it! Certainly, an extraordinary capability for self-introspection exists at the very core of our being. This mental faculty allows humans to experience and evaluate a large variety of abstract concepts—good and evil, right and wrong, compassion and meanness, as well as pain and pleasure. In addition it leads us to wonder about our world and to assign weighted value judgments to various sensory inputs. It even gives us the ability to predict the outcome of our actions before the actual action is taken.

These examples provide only a small sample of the many facets and dimensions associated with the concept of self-awareness. Contemporary views of what it means to be fully human encompass an even broader range of abilities that have been identified and, to some extent, even quantified. But it makes me wonder: Are we sure we have identified them all?

Conscience and Consciousness

One of the most fundamental features of all living things is the ability to interact/communicate in some manner, and this communication is embodied in a simple concept.* From the simplest bacteria to complex mammals, including humans, the primary language of life is touch. All life at some level employs physical contact and/or chemical binding mechanisms to initiate and propagate a living state. And for the simplest single-celled organisms of our world, this rudimentary communication scheme alone appears to be adequate to support physical life.

In contrast, more complex multicellular life forms present a new challenge to biological communication, survival, and development. Their significantly larger size, different cell types, and coordinated biological systems require more sophisticated ways to rapidly sense, process, and respond to a variety of external stimuli. Virtually all advanced life forms possess exquisitely intricate systems of interconnected and communicating cells and tissues. These systems are called neural networks, or nervous systems.

Utilizing unbelievably sensitive and responsive electrical and chemical circuits, the specialized cells of the nervous system are able to communicate with other nerve cells. In addition, they also communicate productively with other cell types. By doing so, they sense changes in the environment and respond in ways that promote the organism's prospects for survival and continued development.

These sensory signals and responses are processed at staggering speeds. For example, nerve impulses in the human body travel at the rate of 130 meters (about 400 feet) per second or nearly 300 miles per hour. This rate would theoretically allow a nerve impulse to traverse the entire human body from head to toe about sixty-five times each second.

*Biologically, this interaction must occur at several levels. On one level, there must be a mechanism allowing molecules of a cell to communicate with each other so the cells can maintain the characteristics of life. Second, communication and interaction between different types of cells within the same organism are necessary. Third, cells or organisms must possess mechanisms to monitor and respond to other cells and to changes in their external environment. Finally, living organisms must be able to interact and/or communicate with one another.

Most highly advanced organisms have gone even further: They have developed elegant and integrated nervous systems and a centralized brain structure consisting of billions of specialized neurons. Lightning fast communication allows advanced biological organisms, including humans, to survive and even thrive because they can respond rapidly and adapt to environmental changes. Not surprisingly, only the most advanced life forms possess such specialized capabilities.

These stimulus/response capabilities are essential survival tools for sophisticated living things, but there are additional and even more important roles for the nervous system. One essential feature is their ability to process large amounts of information and almost instantaneously make weighted judgments concerning the best responses for each situation. The responses must then be executed appropriately.

For example, when we are frightened, how will we respond? Will we run, or stay and fight—and to what extent and in what manner?

These multiple decisions are literally made in a flash, and to accomplish such complex tasks requires enormous mental processing power. Without such abilities, human beings and most other life forms would have a difficult time surviving in this world.

But there is more. The brain and nervous system play even greater roles beyond this awesome raw computing power. One of these roles is the creation of the unique feature we call our consciousness, or self-awareness. As discussed earlier in the chapter, the faculties of overt consciousness and self-awareness advance life to a whole new plane and dimension of existence. Humans possess these faculties in a highly developed state, but they are less apparent or nonexistent in other living things.

In addition, human consciousness and self-awareness embody the concept of conscience. And in many ways, our conscience is what truly motivates and powers us from within. Conscience provides the ability to attach values to our responses—to discern right from wrong, experience guilt, and predict and understand the consequences of our responses. In short, it is one of the most advanced characteristics of life on the planet. And as remarkable as it may seem, it appears to be the exclusive possession of human beings.

The mind, consciousness, and our conscience are incredible yet mysterious facets of humanity. In many ways, we are only beginning to discover the full capabilities and potential that lie within us. Even to this day, the biological mechanisms behind the evolution and development of advanced cognitive abilities such as consciousness and conscience are among the most enigmatic and challenging mysteries in modern biology.[9]

Consciousness, conscience, and self-awareness—are these the ultimate features of biological development? Do these special characteristics make us fully human?

To a significant extent, perhaps they truly do. At least this conclusion appears to be the conventional wisdom in scientific circles. And in some ways, it does seem reasonable. But, once again, I ask the question: Is there something more to us—something so subtle it continues to elude modern scientific dissection?

In reality, we find that the attainment of consciousness and conscience is a bittersweet experience. Along with the ability to contemplate our existence comes the obligation and responsibility to make more difficult decisions regarding our thoughts and actions than ever before. And although conscience and consciousness allow us to experience many new pleasures and satisfactions, we also become vulnerable to a plethora of new pains. These pains are not always of a physical nature. Rather, they involve our emotions, feelings, and deepest heartfelt values. Virtually anyone who has lived and experienced life long enough can attest that the pain associated with conscience and consciousness can easily rival the physical pains we routinely encounter.

Nevertheless, though pain and suffering are occasionally a part of life, to the Random Designer the formation of consciousness and conscience in humans is still a magnificent and monumental triumph! Beginning with the simplest biochemical reactions and building upon the resulting structures and assemblies, the Random Designer has brought forth a most spectacular creation.

So now what? With the advent of evolutionary advancements in biology resulting in the human characteristics of consciousness, conscience, and self-awareness, are the random design principles that guided and directed biology for hundreds of millions of years now obsolete?

Certainly not! Random design is still vitally important. Out of necessity, remnants of randomness will always remain an integral part of the miracle of life, accomplishing great good in the process. Higher-level biological development is clearly at work here. For the first time, at least a few pathways influencing biological development can now be individually monitored and chosen rather than waiting to be randomly discovered. From this point in time and for the foreseeable future, biology need no longer be totally blind! *More importantly, in the whole history of life on the planet, one of God's creations can at least partially perceive its place in nature and actively participate in the determination of its own destiny.*

It is difficult to predict the full consequences of such a significant paradigm shift in biological development, especially in human beings. In a very real sense, the details of the whole process are being worked out this very minute within each of us as we live, breathe, think, and choose. However, one thing appears quite certain: Once human beings developed a discerning consciousness and conscience, life on our planet would never be the same.

There can be no doubt that we live in a complex world where questions abound. This fact challenges and inspires us to continue probing the limits of the unknown in a search for physical *and* spiritual understanding. Nevertheless, with this new sense of awareness, humanity achieved an important milestone. Upon this foundation, mankind is now equipped to begin to discern and fulfill the higher purposes of the Random Designer.

So once again, the story is being told. It is the story of a Creator and the birth of all humanity, beginning with one individual named Adam. Undoubtedly, the story has eternally significant meanings and purposes to convey to us. Will they be appropriately perceived? Will we, as His created human beings, individually and collectively recognize our full potential and privileged place in this world?

To this question the Random Designer says, "Have faith! The privilege is a precious gift and birthright for everyone. It must simply be acknowledged and claimed."

Eyes to See—Ears to Hear—Minds to Perceive

Achieving God Awareness

13

Many years ago, I read an interesting article describing how human beings frequently fail to perceive things that are around them.

The thought stuck with me over the years as I experienced this phenomenon first-hand. Occasionally, people or things just do not register even though I am looking right at them. The problem usually manifests itself in small things, such as when I am searching for an item of clothing or a tool that is not where I think it should properly be located. Typically the item is there, but for some reason, I just miss it. This inability to "see" can be quite a discouraging thing at times. The only consolation that I have discovered is that after years of observing others in a variety of roles, it seems quite clear that the inability to perceive the obvious is not a deficiency peculiar to me. It appears to be a universal human affliction!

Small comfort perhaps, but I have an idea of how it comes about. You see, the mechanism of sight does not occur in the eyes: Seeing is in the mind. Specialized light receptor cells of the retina receive and respond to various wavelengths of light by sending out differential nerve impulses to the brain. These impulses correspond to the light's intensity and color, but on their own the impulses make no sense. They must be processed and meaningfully assembled in the brain. Consequently, if the mind somehow fails to register an object, it becomes in essence, invisible.

To illustrate this concept to my students, I have on occasion conducted an impromptu classroom test of observational abilities. I ask the students to look all around the room and take careful note of every blue-colored item.

"After one minute, we will determine who has the best observation, discernment, and memorization skills," I explain.

The next minute is quite interesting to watch as the students self-consciously look each other over in their diligent quest to seek out all blue objects in the room. After sixty seconds of hasty surveillance and mental cramming, I ask them to stop, look at me, and answer my next question. Smiling, I pause for a few moments, then say, "Now tell me, how many *red-colored objects* did you see?"

There is usually a moment of hesitation and silence as the unexpected question registers in their minds. The pause is quickly followed by a combination of good-natured groans and grins as class members realize what happened. Even though red-colored objects are typically prominent in the room, their search for blue seems to make the red items invisible: Virtually no one ever "sees" them.

So how is it possible that human beings, with highly advanced intelligence and unbelievable information-processing powers, are able to so easily miss the obvious?

One explanation may be related to an inherent limitation of the human consciousness. The human mind is clearly capable of juggling a large number of ideas and thoughts. For example, a young mother can somehow prepare a meal, engage her husband in conversation, settle an argument between two siblings, and plan the rest of the evening for the family—apparently simultaneously and with remarkable ease and effectiveness. But outward appearances can be deceiving: Things are not quite as clear-cut as they may seem. In actuality, our minds do not perform these tasks simultaneously. From a practical perspective, the mind can truly focus on only one conscious thought or idea at a time. This fact is vividly illustrated by an elegant set of scientific experiments.[1-4]

Human subjects, placed in a dark room and "wired" with electrodes to measure brain activity, are tested to correlate what they "see" with corresponding brain activity. A subject views a lighted screen composed of red horizontal bars and green vertical bars interwoven with one another. Scientists then place glasses on the subject. One lens allows only red light to enter; the other lens allows only green light to enter. With the glasses in place, both horizontal and vertical lines are visible, but the conscious brain cannot deal with these dual inputs simultaneously so it oscillates between the two colors, consciously seeing red horizontal bars for an instant and then switching to the green vertical bars at another moment. Thus, it seems that when the mind is confronted with a variety of inputs in real life situations, it does the best it can. It may even go further and assign a weighted value to each individual sensory input, but doing so at such incredible speeds so as to appear instantaneous to us.

This is not to say our minds cannot register multiple inputs. They probably do. An interesting note in this regard is that in the color experiment, even though the human subject consciously sees only one color at a time, the electrodes tell a different story. The subconscious brain is still very much aware of the presence of the other color. It is just not *consciously* aware. Real and visible things in our lives, although readily apparent, may simply fail to be perceived.

As a more practical example, suppose I am trying to watch a ballgame or weather forecast on television while also listening attentively to the words of my wife. In this situation, the stage is set for a significant relational problem to develop. Even if I am genuinely intent on hearing the complete messages of my wife and the television, I invariably fail. If I do not give my undivided attention to one input or the other, something is always missed. To gain the full value and import from the most important source (you know which one), I must deliberately and consciously disengage the other source.

This phenomenon has a logical consequence: *Unless we are actively looking or listening for something, there is a real and distinct possibility it will simply fail to reach our conscious awareness, at least not at the levels that are desired.*

In a broader sense, this limited awareness may lead to a perception of the world that is limited or significantly skewed from reality.

Such thoughts bring several questions to mind: Is it possible that we might be failing to perceive something vital in our current definitions of what it means to be fully human? What if the Creator is waiting for us to discover and cultivate a completely different and previously unknown feature that is a part of us—an awareness meant exclusively for us?

This may be the case, or it may not. However, if it is true, then the ideas I have shared in this chapter possess a powerful and practical significance: They suggest this special awareness will only be perceived if we attentively and purposefully look for it. Perhaps the Random Designer has used humanity's advanced cognitive capacities to accomplish this very goal—to bring His most special creation to an awareness of Himself.

In this light, and as incredible as it may seem on the surface, all the cold, impersonal scientific laws and principles of physics, chemistry, and biology presented in this book are nothing more than a backdrop to a much larger and more significant reality. These laws and principles have simply provided the raw materials and a framework to sequentially and systematically assemble higher order biological structure and function. Now, after a long and literally unfathomable period of time and extended effort, random design principles have successfully completed the purpose for which they were originally intended. And indeed it is an amazing accomplishment! Finally, for the first time in the long and arduous history of all created life, the ultimate purpose of the Random Designer begins to come to fruition: *The created can now perceive the Creator.*

Maybe this is what it really means to be fully human—to not only be self-aware, but also God-aware! Of course, such a suggestion is a difficult and mystical concept for the world of experimental biology. It offers scant opportunity for scientific validation or confirmation. In fact, it may be completely outside the domain of scientific study—at least for the time being. And although scientists and non-scientists alike may hotly debate the point for a long time, there can be no doubt that we are exceedingly more than just our chemistry.

Who knows? This unique characteristic of God-awareness may be the key that helps us better understand ourselves and our ultimate purposes. After all, here we are—intelligent human beings created from the chaotic forces of randomness. And we find ourselves at this particular place and time as the apparent pinnacle of all that has ever been created.

Now, with eyes that see, ears that hear, and minds capable of perceiving the existence of God, each of us can begin to understand His mysterious ways.

An Honest Faith

Discerning God's Fingerprints

14

The proposition that there really is a God or a Master Designer is not a scientific conclusion. As discussed previously, science cannot ultimately prove or disprove God's existence. Scientific observation and analysis may provide many useful insights, but in the final analysis, the question reduces itself to a matter of personal faith—an individual decision to believe or not to believe a Creator really does exist. If we do indeed believe in God, then, by implication, it would seem that a design element should be apparent in our world.

So what is this design and what are the Creator's purposes? Are they complicated and difficult, or are they simple to perceive and comprehend? Our systematic search for answers to guide and direct us generally finds corporate expression in the body of organized religion. So is religion where we find the answers?

Unfortunately, the jury is still out on this question. In our current science-driven culture, conservative religious proponents are sometimes seen as narrow-minded and anti-intellectual. While I have not found this perception to be entirely accurate, I must concede that at times such portrayals are not totally undeserved. For some religious people, it is simply far too tempting to automatically attribute anything that is not easily understood to a supernatural cause and to inappropriately interpret scripture as a literal scientific textbook.

Although these responses often cast religion in a negative light, in my view they are not sufficient to discount religious faith overall. Organized religion still offers great value, especially when promoting avenues through which we might discover God.

Realistically, today's society grants a high level of authority to both science *and* religion. With this understanding in mind, it seems important to discern when it is appropriate to integrate these two disciplines. Above all, if one's primary goal is to discover a vital relationship with God as opposed to defending some particular religious or scientific turf, then anxiety, fear, or hostility toward one another should completely vanish. Our common goal is to discover God's truth and find His purposes for our lives.

Sometimes I wonder if our noble and enthusiastic attempts to give God our full devotion lead us to occasionally draw overly simplistic conclusions about Him—especially regarding His nature and what He considers to be of greatest importance. If this is the case, two logical and concurrent outcomes seem likely. First, our own personal spiritual development will be hindered; and second, we will convey to others incomplete or inaccurate concepts of God.

For example, when speaking of the origin and development of living beings, some believe that they must defend God from the secular intrusion of atheism. They insist that He *supernaturally* (apart from natural laws) created life exactly as portrayed in the Bible—*literally from nothing*. But I wonder if God is more ingenious than that. After all, is this supernatural description of creation truly any more miraculous than God using the raw material of His creative genius to establish life over billions of years? Both methods seem laudable and God-like to me.

In another defense of God scenario, someone may assert, for instance, that God worked a miraculous physical healing in his or her life, or in the life of another. This event might be proclaimed to all as proof of God's existence and power. The contention might be voiced overtly, or it might be conveyed in a more subtle manner. I most often hear it expressed something like this: "It had to be a miracle—there is no other explanation."

I am always puzzled at such words, for they no doubt reveal more about the individual who is speaking than about God. I suspect these people really mean that they, or their medical professional, cannot understand how things could possibly have turned out so well, and they are naturally thankful. And such a response is understandable. Whenever someone is restored from illness to physical health, a feeling of gratitude is certainly appropriate, regardless of the mechanism by which it occurred. But can we be truly frank with one another? *Just because a physical event is unexplained, does not automatically make it supernatural.* A person may believe supernatural forces were responsible, however without some sort of validation, it remains only a belief, and it does not necessarily prove God's existence.

Please do not misunderstand. Most people, myself included, would love to embrace the idea of routine supernatural healing. Have an ailment or disease? Get on your knees, pray earnestly, and voilà—healed! You have to admit, it is an appealing concept. But it seems to me that we must be consistent in our appraisals of cause and effect. The truth of the matter is that God does not always grant physical healing even when requested by the most devout. And herein lies the danger for many individuals who profess strong religious convictions.

If one claims that a physical healing is accomplished supernaturally by God, and that this healing proves His existence, then what conclusion is to be drawn when physical health is not restored? Certainly, if a consistent standard is applied, this negative result could lead one to conclude that God does not exist. Similarly, if religious position holds that a "supernatural" 10,000-year-old earth with all life coming into being in six twenty-four hour days is the ultimate proof of God's power and presence, what effect does compelling scientific evidence demonstrating the implausibility of these claims do to belief in God?

From my observation, religion is typically eager to embrace scientific evidence that supports a particular religious idea, but even-handed application of this principle is not uniformly observed. When scientific findings cast doubt on a widely held religious view, scientific input usually gets the quick boot. Thus, science is perceived as good when it supports a religious claim, but is often portrayed as pure evil when it does not.

The truth is that we simply cannot have it both ways. When people make broad and definitive claims regarding the physical world based upon a few isolated experiences, testimonials, or questionable scriptural interpretations, these claims must be uniformly borne out by broader objective observation. If the claims cannot be readily verified, then they must be open to question and even direct challenge. Religious faith that refuses to allow sincere questioning or challenge is a fragile faith at best. It will be difficult to ever reliably establish its value and genuineness

With these thoughts in mind, it seems to me that individuals of religious faith have a sobering responsibility. *There is a real, albeit inadvertent risk, that in the earnest desire to promote God in every possible way, reason may be left behind. The effect is that people of faith may find themselves unintentionally diminishing the image of God in the eyes of others, while simultaneously compromising their own credibility to speak for Him on this and other important issues of life. They will be automatically discounted, if not totally dismissed.*

This discussion is not meant to suggest that supernatural interventions relating to the physical world are impossible. I personally believe that an individual's faith in God can positively and effectively intertwine with physical responses. I raise this issue of the physical and the supernatural mainly because I believe God respects an honest searching faith that heeds *all* of the signs that point to Him. If we view Him simplistically as a magician in the sky who suspends His own physical laws at a whim, I wonder if we honor the full extent of His creativeness properly. Are we really seeing Him as He is, or as we would like Him to be? And if He really is more creative than we previously supposed, maybe deeper insights into His creative nature are available for us to discover.

The points of this chapter ultimately reduce to a couple of relatively simple and fundamental questions. First, are the many superficial physical things upon which we disproportionately focus our attention—such as physical health—truly in congruence with the Creator's primary purposes and plans? For the most part, I have my doubts.

Second, do we really think God needs one of His creation's feeble attempts to defend Him in order to prove His existence? To some extent, perhaps we really do believe this is the case. But is it not also true that we are usually far more interested in proving our own particular version of God than we are in defending God Himself?

Honestly, it seems so silly. Surely, the Creator of the universe possesses ample ability to authenticate Himself to His world without our meager and frequently misguided assistance. Indeed, if we realistically probe the depths of His creation extensively—looking beyond the easy explanations, I believe we find that He has already revealed Himself in many, many ways. His fingerprints are on all of His created order.

No doubt, the world is a mysterious and wonderful place. As we seek guidance, it is my sincere desire that we will not only discover deeper levels of understanding and spiritual experience, but that we will also learn to more effectively exercise our faith in honest, genuine, and credible ways.

In His Image

A New Paradigm for Living

15

The Biblical account of creation portrays man as being made in the image of God. This, of course, raises immediate and legitimate questions regarding the precise meaning of this concept. From the standpoint of our current discussion, the question is of utmost relevance. For if we are truly created in the image of God, this implies we might actually mirror Him in many ways. Therefore, in a manner of speaking, this concept gets right to the heart of what God might really be like.

Most individuals would readily concur that the image of God probably is not a literal physical image. Indeed, from a biological perspective, if the image of God were a direct reflection of outward physical features, it would be difficult to attribute this special characteristic only to humans. For instance, in advanced biological beings such as animals and humans, the essential physical organization and physiology are built upon similar themes. Muscle tissue and bones within different animals and humans possess remarkable regularity in their basic form. Also, major organs such as the heart, liver, spleen, lungs, and pancreas from different species possess comparable corresponding design and carry out their functions in basically the same manner. Thus, on a large scale and from a strictly *physical* point of view, human beings are not all that special compared to many other advanced life forms.

In contrast to this large-scale view, at more detailed levels, including cognitive functions and other invisible elements of life, it is easy to see that humans are indeed *very* special. In fact, random design has generated virtually infinite numbers of subtle physical variations in the basic biological scheme of things, ultimately giving each living being its own individual uniqueness.

Therefore, if we accept the view that being made in the image of God is a characteristic accredited solely to humans, and also that it is not a physical image, then what is it? Is it a spiritual image? Is it a reflection of our mental conscience and consciousness? How can we really understand this concept?

The Mind of God

As we have seen from earlier chapters, by systematically and methodically using physical laws and materials, the Random Designer elevated His biological creation to increasingly complex levels of organization and structure. This incredible and unlikely process appears to have culminated with us—the most magnificent of His creations. The one special and distinctive feature that truly sets humans apart from all other living creatures appears to be our extraordinary minds. Thus, on a relative scale, all the physical/athletic attributes we so greatly admire and esteem, actually hold little real consequence or value, except as they serve to promote physical survival and support our most essential mental capacities. Thus, the logical conclusion appears to be quite clear: To be created in the image of God means to have a mind like God.

This thought encompasses several possible features including, among others, our conscious awareness, our conscience, universally shared concepts of right and wrong, and an inborn desire for connection and relationship.

Recall from chapter six that a living cell or organism is ultimately a product of the specific proteins it makes, and that the proteins of a cell are a direct reflection of its genes. Thus, it appears that over eons, the genetic constitution of human beings has attained a sufficiently advanced level of complexity and organization to synthesize and support a truly superior mental capacity—the human brain. The human brain may be the ultimate biological faculty, possessing the ability to perceive and process things in ways other living creatures cannot achieve or comprehend. Who knows? The human brain may even possess capabilities and communication potential we ourselves have not yet fathomed—especially as it relates to our communication with the Creator Himself.

This idea does raise interesting and perhaps disconcerting scientific questions. For example, since human beings and chimpanzees possess nearly 98% similarity in their gene structure, it seems logical to wonder which genes might be responsible for the higher cognitive development of humans. In a simplistic way of thinking, these genes would become primary candidates to be heralded as "Mind of God" genes. But of course, as with so many scientific questions, this approach is far too simple and naive. Biological interactions are much more complicated. Indeed, geneticists and developmental biologists continue to be amazed at how different genes, as well as their corresponding proteins, interact with each other in enormously sophisticated and as yet, poorly understood ways. Such complex gene/protein interactions are able to generate dramatically different biological structure and function from a relatively limited repertoire of gene differences: Just a few key gene changes can account for astounding variation in biological, mental, and cognitive makeup. In addition, the cumulative and dynamic effects of existing genes acting cooperatively and productively with each other must also be considered. The truth is that brain organization, connection and communication giving rise to consciousness are great unknowns in biology. Consequently, the "Image of God" concept is likely to be a much more involved matter than simply identifying a few unique or specialized genes. And it seems that dramatic new insights are unlikely to materialize anytime soon

But even though we do not wholly understand the precise mechanisms by which the "Image of God" comes about in us, it seems clear that the concept must hold some validity. Therefore, it would seem useful to focus our attention on the potential opportunities and benefits that might accrue to us as a consequence. The primary characteristic of the mind of God must certainly be distinguishable in some way from the mind of man.

The Survival Paradigm—Selfishness

It seems quite evident that human beings, at least for the present, are the culmination of the magnificent random design creative process. And while I suspect that some evolutionary scientists might strongly debate the implications of such a statement, it is difficult to deny that we are truly special creatures of His creation. But we are not most special because of our physical nature. I believe our most profound quality is our unique aptitude for sensing God. Further, being made in the image of God might even lead to higher levels of sensing Him than just a vague awareness of His existence.

Capabilities such as these seem to go far beyond what biologists might predict from an understanding of biochemistry, genetics, development, and evolution. In fact, these sensing capabilities actually appear to have catapulted humanity to a level that in many ways transcends the predictability inherent in the laws of biochemistry and physics.

However, while the random design elements of biology are essential to all life, having brought us to our current state, these random design principles also have significant built-in limitations.

As previously stated, the primary and virtually universal driving force of all biology, even as applied to mankind, appears to be physical survival. For better or worse, squarely embedded at the epicenter of this survival instinct is the behavioral element of selfishness, or self-centeredness. While selfish behavior is not routinely viewed in a positive light, we have seen that it is a key component of biological survival—an essential and core element of all life. Thus, in terms of physical survival, selfishness is a positive: It breeds success.

I am fully aware that using the word selfishness may be somewhat confusing, since it attributes a human-defined behavioral characteristic to fundamental biological processes. Other words might be appropriately substituted to convey a similar meaning. However, in the current context, I think the word selfishness will suffice. Selfishness is the idea of putting one's self first and foremost virtually all the time. And in this strict connotation, an animal, or even individual cells or cell components could exhibit selfish behavior without being aware. This survival instinct, or selfishness, is the primary makeup of the mind of man, indeed of all life. Directly or indirectly, it impacts virtually every aspect of life on this planet.

It is easy to find examples of selfish behavior in a biological context. Animals fighting over food in predator-prey interactions or people battling for the accumulation of power and material wealth are clear examples. On a much smaller biological level, viruses and cancer cells are the most notable examples of selfish entities.

Viruses are the ultimate parasites, meeting all their needs by mercilessly infecting and usurping the resources of their targeted host cells. Cancer cells, on the other hand, exhibit a much more subtle and insidious type of selfish behavior. Following several damaging mutations, cancer cells go awry, escaping the regulatory controls that typically govern normal non-cancerous cells. The result is that they grow uncontrollably, thriving at the expense of adjacent normal cells by hoarding essential nutrients and other growth factors.

Ironically, neither viruses nor cancer cells make any conscious effort to behave in this fashion. It is just the way they are genetically programmed to survive. In their selfish quest for immortality, for both unchecked viral infections and rampant unrestrained cancer cell growth, the fate is the same—ultimate destruction of not only the host organism, but the selfish entities as well.

These two examples illustrate the negative impact that invariably arises from selfish behaviors in biology. But as we have seen, this is not always the case. Under "normal" circumstances the selfish driving force of biology can also accomplish great good. For eons, through the mutation/selection process, it has successfully formulated the biological background and established the necessary framework for biological synthesis reactions—ultimately paving a pathway for the emergence and endurance of life, and even humankind.

But now it appears that the innate selfish biological nature has taken life as far as is possible. Without a new paradigm for living, human beings, along with all other forms of life, would be forever constrained by the primal instincts of survival and propagation. Even at its best, such an existence would be most unsatisfying.

If survival and the physical essence of our existence are all there is to life, then the potential for us to experience true meaning, purpose, and satisfaction would not really extend much further than that seen in an amoeba, a fruit fly, or a dog. So is there really a better way? And if so, what is it and how can it be attained? How can we break free of these rigid biological constraints?

A New Paradigm—Selflessness

The pathway that frees humanity from these physical/biological bonds appears to be a paradox. Everything in biology uniformly conveys the message that random design and survival of the fittest, or "self first," are the universal governing standards for all life. The paradox is that this new and higher calling for humanity is totally different: It actually places *others above self*. Thus, as its most central feature, the new paradigm functions in a manner that is actually contrary to the selfish creative forces of survival and random design—those very elements of biology that brought it into existence in the first place.

The new paradigm is selflessness. This concept recognizes that significant value can sometimes accrue when the interests of another are put ahead of one's own. The thought is certainly not a new one, but is critical for us to comprehend and embrace its full import. In many ways selfless benevolent action appears to be the defining gold standard and representation of what it means to be a human being made in the image of God. Human acquisition of this different mind-set spawns a dawning realization within our minds that newfound powers and previously untapped potential are now within our grasp.

Deeper levels of discernment and potential experience become possible for humanity. In addition, as these senses are recognized, developed, and more regularly integrated into our individual and collective lives, a subtle but expanding personal awareness begins to take shape in our minds. We gradually come to recognize that selfless behavior really can be constructive—elevating humankind above the basic inborn and constitutional rules of biology. As a consequence, we, as human beings, can establish a new course of existence for our world, that transcends all previous models.

Most importantly, selflessness empowers us to manage our lives in ways that are in stark contrast to all other life on the planet. Human beings, alone among all God's living creations, have the power to directly repudiate the congenital commands of life's biological survival program—they can say no to selfish behavior!

In a very real sense, all of humanity today is challenged to rise above the primal existence of the animals. Noble principles of existence can now be valued and promoted over the simple pragmatics of everyday life.

Human beings have acquired a subtle but powerful life-changing tool that no other living creature on our planet has ever possessed. It is the tool of choice—the privilege and grand opportunity to purposely select non-selfish behavior over self-centered behavior. And in a most phenomenal way, in doing so, each of us is offered a brand new beginning as we personally begin to experience and comprehend the enormous potential wrapped up in this simple, but priceless gift.

To be sure, on the surface, and certainly for the short-term, saying no to selfish behavior might appear to be counterproductive. Our modern secular world places tremendous value upon competition, survival of the fittest, and satisfaction of individual desires. From such a perspective, this selflessness paradigm may be difficult to understand. In fact, many people will categorically reject it, precisely because the immediate consequences do not appear to be in their own self-interest. And in a way, such responses are valid: When considering straightforward biological/physical contexts, selfish value systems do appear to work best in most cases, at least for the short term. But all is not as it seems.

> Human beings have it within their power to directly repudiate the congenital commands of life's biological survival program—they can say no to selfish behavior!

People who live their lives solely according to self-centered precepts do not fully comprehend the consequences of their short-sightedness. They fail to see that the biological/scientific principles supporting the values upon which they have established their lives were and are designed for application to the physical world only. When applied to the highest levels of human experience, areas such as personal satisfaction and spiritual fulfillment, the self-centered biological rules of life simply do not work the same way. They return to the person empty and void.

But if there is no immediate or visible reward for a selfless lifestyle, then what are the real benefits and values for living by such a seemingly unnatural code? Intuitively, I suspect each of us already knows the answer to this question. In fact, it is not a new idea at all. The words have been spoken many times before in many different ways, but perhaps we have not fully recognized their deeper meaning:

"Among you, it is different."

"He who wants to be the greatest must be a servant."

"Greater love has no man, than he give up his life for a friend."

"Do unto others as you would have them do unto you."

"It is better to give than to receive."

These and similar selfless thoughts reflect the mind of God. In some ways, this concept of selfless living may appear somewhat mystical because it cannot be easily verified by science. Nevertheless, I believe almost everyone can understand its intrinsic significance. We all know and understand the warm feeling that fills us when we do something good for someone else with no thought of reward. We are also acutely aware of the penetrating and intense pain that accompanies an act of selfishness or betrayal. The fundamental truth and value of the concept appears to be ingrained within the very core of our consciousness. Because of this fact, something even more remarkable becomes possible.

Love and Relationships

When mankind finally arrived at that special point in time, perhaps tens of thousands of years ago, and became truly God-aware for the first time, this realization was probably accompanied by a whole new array of discernment capabilities. Amidst all these attributes, one of particular importance appears to stand out from all of the others. By utilizing the newly acquired behavioral option of selflessness, humankind developed the capacity to discover and experience genuine love and relationship.

I believe you will agree with me that love and relationships are supreme and universally cherished values among human beings.

They represent the antithesis to selfishness and the instincts of basic biological survival. In fact, without the capacity to put another's interests ahead of our own, mutually satisfying and fulfilling relationships are virtually impossible.

Consequently, it seems to me the Creator might be speaking a very important message to us. It is an invitation to become more like Him by putting aside self-centered and selfish lifestyles. In doing so, we gradually discover that none of us can learn what He is really like unless we first break free of the basic biological survival program which holds us prisoner in this physical world.

A selfless lifestyle certainly does not mean we should allow everyone we meet to trample on us, or that we should deny the reality of our physical and biological ties. Our physical desires and connections are very real, strong, and even essential. However, it does mean we must clearly acknowledge one important fact: *Selfishness and the behaviors associated with selfishness do not mirror the mind of God.*

There is no doubt that to a large extent we are captive to the physical world and the fundamental rules of biology—those necessary, special and unique, but often brutal forces that have nurtured the survival of our species for eons. Yet despite these strong biological cables that bind us, hindering us from reaching our full potential, there remains within a keen awareness and an undying hope that we were made for something better—a compelling inner conviction that we, as God's special creation, can rise above our biological limitations and discover a reality that extends beyond what we see, feel, hear, smell, and taste.

The biological bonds of selfishness can be broken! And when they are successfully overcome, we as human beings are granted the most wonderful and mystical privilege—the opportunity to establish vital, dynamic, and satisfying relationships with others, and even more significantly, with God.

Created for Connection

Acknowledging God

16

I remember the vivid event as if it were only yesterday, although twenty-six years have passed since the arrival of our very first son. Everything happened so fast. It started with a positive pregnancy test for my wife, Sally. The test was followed by regular prenatal visits to the doctor, horse-sized vitamin pills, regular physical exercise, baby showers, a baby crib, and lots of tender loving care from the father-to-be. The weeks and months went by like a blur. Then, before we knew it, he was here.

As he gasped for his first breath in this new world, I saw his bright eyes light up with life and energy. He did not cry, but rather whimpered softly as the doctor passed him to the kind delivery room nurse, who then placed this brand new human creation into the waiting and loving arms of an incredulous young mother. Our emotions in that moment were overpowering. Though Sally was totally spent physically, all the discomfort and pain preceding the delivery instantly vanished from her face. "Look at my baby! Look at my baby! Oh, look at my beautiful, beautiful baby!" She exclaimed over and over and over again. As I looked into her soft blue eyes, tears streamed like torrents down our smiling faces. Gently, I held the arm of this beautiful new mother as we gazed in awe upon this tiny creation we had just brought into the world—our first son, Jeremiah, a miraculous mixture of us.

The powerful images of that day are burned indelibly into my memory and consciousness. They are so vivid that even now, after all these years, the emotions of that rainy morning in October return to me in full force as I think and write about them.

Needless to say, that day marked the beginning of many changes for Sally and me. Suddenly, it seemed we spent every minute of every day wrapped up in the life of this little "bundle of joy." We fed him, changed his diapers, and talked to him, bouncing, playing, and laughing on the floor for hours on end. In the evenings, we would take turns gently rocking him in our little orange rocking chair until his eyelids began to droop, and he slowly drifted off to sleep.

In the following weeks and months, we, like most parents, were anxious for our son to discover himself, his potential—and also us. Jeremiah's mind developed quickly as his awareness of his surroundings expanded. At first, Sally and I were merely moving objects that caught his attention from across the room. However, with time we realized he was also developing the ability to discern us as distinct individuals. In addition, not only did he recognize us; he also learned he could trust us—choosing to be held in our arms over the arms of a stranger.

Later, when Jeremiah approached the age where he would begin to speak, there was great anticipation and banter between Sally and me as to whose name he would say first. One evening shortly thereafter, as we rolled and played on the floor, Jeremiah unexpectedly looked up into my eyes and spoke his very first word. You know what it was. It was that mystical word of connection every father waits to hear from his son or daughter from the moment they are born. DaDa!

Well actually, it was more like Da-Da-Da-Da-Da—and he did get just a wee bit of coaxing. You know what I am saying. Nonetheless, he had called my name for the very first time. And before long, he had made the firm connection—pointing his finger in my direction and loudly proclaiming me to the world as his father.

I remember feeling an overwhelming sense of responsibility and completeness that I had never before experienced or even dreamed possible. My very own creation—my son—knew who I was, could call me by name and most of all, wanted to be identified with me. It seemed that a whole new perspective of the world was unfolding before me. I sensed feelings of fulfillment, connection, and purpose that were beyond description. You who are fathers and mothers know exactly what I mean. Even now, you are reminiscing and recalling with fondness those special times of first recognition with your own children. They are unforgettable events to be treasured. The memory of this momentous milestone in our lives will never depart from my consciousness! At that precise instant, this father realized he would never stop loving his boy.

But of course, just because my son knew I existed and that I was his father did not mean he even remotely understood the full significance of this newly discovered relationship. How could he possibly grasp such a complicated concept at such an early age? In a very real sense, he will need a lifetime of experience and learning to attain the perspective of his father.

Nevertheless, perceiving and acknowledging is an important first step. At that precise moment and forever after, the potential for a continuously growing awareness, connection, and relationship between father and son became possible. It was a brand new beginning—the start of a vital, dynamic, and eternal bond.

Connecting with the Creator

In like manner, it seems to me we are all created for a similar special purpose. When each of us first perceives and then acknowledges our Creator-father, we fulfill a destiny that, although somewhat mystical, is no less real. Choosing to follow Him leads to a whole lifetime of listening and learning, as we attempt to effectively discern His presence, priorities, and purposes for our lives. In this sense, truly discovering God is as much a *process* as an instantaneous revelation. And like all strong relationships, it is a process that takes time. On a grand scale then, perhaps the creation account of Adam is really the beginning of an ongoing story—a never-ending quest of humankind to find the Creator and acquire meaningful answers to questions that began to well up within the consciousness of the early human mind many thousands of years ago.

If this innate desire to find God is the primary directive and goal of our existence, then it seems to me that two parallel realities may be unfolding in our world, each played out at different levels, but concurrently in time. One reality is a collective portrait of humanity's long and ongoing struggle for physical survival, as well as our continuing search for meaning and purpose in the midst of a sometimes harsh and chaotic world. The other reality, while encompassing similar goals to the first, is much more personal—only to be experienced on an individual basis in the mind and soul of each of us during our brief tenure on this planet.

But there is even more to consider, for these distinct realities are not necessarily disconnected. What happens in the personal arena can also have profound effects upon the total human experience. Each of us may actually be unknowing, but potentially important figures in a much larger cast of characters.

Biology provides many examples of this concept in action. In our bodies, hundreds of cells perform unique and specialized functions which, when working properly, individually and collectively contribute to our overall well-being. While each cell type is only one among thousands, they are all critically important. For instance, pancreas cells possess the specialized ability to produce the hormone insulin. Red blood cells are another example, carrying oxygen to all parts of the body. Thus, each body cell has a unique and important job, and when each one reliably carries out its given task the body remains healthy and alive.

In a similar manner, each of us has unique characteristics and potential. And when these abilities are exercised to their fullest, we too play important roles in molding and shaping the future of our world. More succinctly, the decisions and actions of a single person really can have a significant positive impact and contribute to the larger scheme of things.

But how do we discover our individual roles, and how do we ascertain who we really are and what we can become? Realistically, I believe we all know the answer to this question. We sense that only one source can provide the most authoritative answer. So we wonder when that magical moment will arrive for us—that special moment when we come face-to-face with our Creator, speak His name, and personally begin the process of learning our unique and particular purposes in this life.

Fortunately, I do not believe God is hiding. In fact, I am coming to believe that His presence and workings in our world are much more pervasive than generally perceived. But I also believe there are some very real reasons for our failure to sense Him.

After many years spent living and working in the domain of scientific research and university education and experiencing day-to-day life like everyone else, I have concluded that we may actually be looking right past Him. Our sights are off. Our radio receiver is tuned to the wrong frequency.

Virtually every day we seek to fulfill the many demands upon our lives—working longer hours, making more money, and accumulating more material goods. Sometimes our plight seems overwhelming. Information and technology seem to be driving us (or more accurately, dragging us) into a swirling vortex of identification numbers, passwords, and trivia cleverly disguised as things that are "important." The ultimate goal of this technology is always the same—to become faster and faster, and increasingly more efficient.

I do not believe God is hiding. In fact, I am coming to believe His presence and workings in our world may be much more pervasive than is generally perceived.

Consider a paraphrase of what Jerry Yang, a co-founder of the well-known internet search engine company Yahoo had to say during a PBS *Frontline* documentary on internet technology.[1] In describing the role of Yahoo and its value to us, he spoke with great insight and clarity: "It helps us waste time faster. That way we don't have to waste time wasting time."

I wonder if he does not have it about right. Inevitably our thirst for information and all the other physical attractions of our world are dictating not only our immediate direction, but also our ultimate destiny. But do they really make us better people?

I, for one, have my doubts.

The truth is that the things of this world do not serve us well when they so preoccupy our minds that we lose sight of what is really most important in life. Success and understanding in these physical arenas of life simply do not satisfy the hunger in our souls.

Notwithstanding, as we are continually inundated with massive amounts of information that reach out and grab us at the speed of light, demanding our attention and energy, the still small voice of God from within simply becomes overwhelmed.

I believe that the heart of the matter is this: When all of the variables of life have been fully evaluated and a pivotal point of decision is reached, we must individually and collectively determine what we will value most. We are created for connection and relationship.

At the very core of our being, we all sense that this is true. Certainly strong love bonds connect a father and his son together through time and adversity, but I am coming to believe this earthly relationship, as fulfilling as it is, pales in comparison to the depth of God's love and concern for us. The first step in any relationship is an acknowledgment. It is not required that we understand the complete nature of our Father or where the relationship will ultimately lead. We can trust God to help us with these aspects. The only initial requirement is that we look up to the heavens in faith and from the depths of our souls sincerely utter those mystical words of recognition and connection: "DaDa."

Cosmic Loneliness

Genetically Wired for God

17

In the previous chapter I suggested we are created for relationships, both with God and each other. This desire for connection is so strong and universal that it sometimes seems there is an actual void existing within our consciousness — a void that can only be best filled by God.

But what force draws us toward the Creator and to a relationship with Him?

Traditional and modern science has difficulty addressing issues of this nature because they fall within a domain called the "soft" sciences. Soft sciences encompass the behavioral disciplines, such as religion, theology, sociology, and psychology. These areas of study are in stark contrast to the "hard" sciences of chemistry and physics. But soft science does not imply that these disciplines are any less significant. In many ways, drawing firm conclusions in the soft sciences is a much greater challenge because the questions typically involve multiple variables, many of which are complex and impossible to completely control. Additionally, studies in the soft sciences frequently entail elements of diverse personal experience.

Biological research, while not quite so imprecise, experiences similar challenges. Subtle biological diversity is built into the very nature of life and makes virtually every biological question a multivariable proposition. In fact, most experimental biologists have learned one lesson very well: Nature has a way of surprising us when we draw definitive conclusions too quickly. Because of this awareness, scientists generally apply great caution to the interpretation and extrapolation of new scientific data. However, though cautious, they recognize that the overall scientific story never fails to materialize in a consistent and coherent way. Consequently, compared to most people, scientists learn to be comfortable with higher levels of uncertainty. They understand that in a complex world, satisfying answers to life's questions are not easy. But even though scientists cannot foresee the final outcome of an investigation, through experience they have learned to trust that the findings will ultimately make sense within a broader scheme. Likewise, many people of strong religious faith follow a similar track. Experience gives them confidence in their overall beliefs and convictions.

It seems likely that when investigating more challenging soft science intangibles, including how God draws us to Himself, totally satisfying scientific explanations may be eternally elusive. But this fact does not negate the genuine nature of God. It just means that science lacks the necessary understanding and investigative tools to study Him at this time.

So how does science grapple with an abstract concept such as loneliness? Loneliness is definitely a challenging concept. In fact, from the perspective of hard science, it may be impossible to prove it even exists. However, the inability of science to address the concept in understandable terms does not diminish the sure and certain fact that loneliness is a very real and genuine part of human existence. Everyone has experienced it in one form or another. And I am sure you will agree that the emotions accompanying loneliness are powerful and extremely convincing.

Similarly, an innate craving for closeness is strong within us. Each of us knows the intense yearning for intimacy and satisfying relationship. And it cries out for a response: *No one wants to be alone!* Therefore, while we may never completely understand the ultimate source and nature of these desires, there can be no doubt that they are a fundamental element of our nature. I even wonder if they might be a mirrored reflection of God Himself.

Some scientists would staunchly maintain that this sense of loneliness and the corresponding desire for connection with others are merely consequences of the biological/survival paradigm. Instead, they would present explanations based on our biological and physical needs for a reliable social fabric: We survive if we cooperate. Therefore, cooperation and the desire for connection are simply evolutionary adaptations. As a scientist I readily concede that such ideas have some merit—at least within appropriate boundaries. But I also wonder if there might be more to this concept than just physical evolution, survival, and perpetuation of one's genes. While interpersonal attraction and desire for relationship between human beings are strong, legitimate, and powerful forces, even the most satisfying human relationships fail to fulfill a deeper hunger in our souls. Thus, the universal desire for relationship appears to extend beyond mere human interaction. Some psychologists and theologians have even coined a name for this desire. They call it "cosmic loneliness." Others have suggested we are "wired for God."

These facts, in association with everything else we know about ourselves, lead me to wonder whether such powerful drives might be part of a more purposeful plan. *Perhaps the Random Designer intentionally created us with minds and psyches that crave these relational connections in order to accomplish a dual purpose—one for biological survival and another to lead His creation to Him.*

Such an intriguing proposition would certainly be challenging to demonstrate experimentally. As mentioned before, the tools of science are not equipped to investigate and validate such nonphysical phenomena. For many, this absence of proof, in and of itself, presents a significant obstacle to a belief in God. We are accustomed to relying primarily upon our physical senses and scientific evidence to define reality for us.

But in spite of our inability to see, touch, or understand God in the physical dimension, we intuitively sense He is real—or at the very least, that He might be real. And the universality of such thoughts among all humankind, even people with little or no formal religious training, suggests something of vital importance that should not be missed.

If we are truly made in the image of God—that is, having His mind-set, then it seems reasonable that we might, at least in part, resemble His image and nature in our most noble desires and behaviors. Of course, this idea raises the intriguing possibility that God may actually have needs and desires. But more importantly it suggests to me that, as in the case of parents and children, His primary desire is to foster a relationship with His creation.

Human relationships, such as a father to his son, may mirror this connection to a degree and I believe that there is a great deal to be learned about the nature of God from these types of relationships. However, human connections do not seem to touch this one. No other person, possession, or power can adequately substitute for a relationship with God. Only He can occupy that special place in our minds. Only He can fully satisfy the deep internal craving to find our unique place in this world. He alone tells us who we really are and what we can become.

So what if it really is true? Maybe the deep longing for relationship and the insatiable appetite for closeness that exists within us is a built-in biological clue. Perhaps it is a cryptic message—a reminder of what it truly means to be a human being made in the image of God. All along scientists have speculated that this hunger for God is simply another random biological/evolutionary adaptation allowing us to address our human frailties and insecurities. But when we summon enough courage to believe, and scrutinize it closely, it begins to look more and more like a doorway to the Creator.

Where Is God, Really?

The Kingdom of God Is Within Us

18

God may make His residence in a far-away galaxy, live outside of the perceived limits of our universe, encompass a whole different physical dimension, or maybe even exist in a manner that escapes our wildest imagination altogether. No one seems to know exactly where He is. When people envision God, they generally think of Him as a powerful being who somehow appears to them in an unknown manner from a distant, but poorly-defined place called heaven. But I wonder sometimes whether this image is really on target—or even close for that matter. Maybe His existence is much more immediate and intimate, even nearer than we could possibly have imagined.

It appears that God may actually reside within, inhabiting us as a core component of our minds. If God does live within us, the suggestion that He resides in our minds is not all that unexpected. After all, where else would He be in the world? Certainly we would not expect to find Him residing in our muscles, bones, or even our vibrant, beating hearts.

Think of it: what an ingenious and efficient mechanism. What a masterful way to make Himself universally available and knowable to every human being!

From our earliest beginnings, humanity has intently projected its gaze outward to the far reaches of our galaxy, searching through space and time for some hint or clue to our origin and identity. How unexpected to find that the object of our search can only be discovered within. In a very real sense, God appears to have embedded Himself deep within the recesses of our minds as the central and core element of our conscious being. And from this center of consciousness He speaks universal truths and standards to all mankind.

For those who adhere to more traditional religious points of view, this idea may sound like yet another attempt to scientifically explain God, thus striking a chord of caution in their wary minds. And then of course, there will always be some scientists—those few who cannot find room for God in any part of their existence—who will either recoil in horror at the thought of God within, or simply shake their heads in disbelief that this "God thing" just refuses to go away.

This God-within concept may seem to be a provocative and novel way to view God; however, in reality, it is not new at all. It has been articulated numerous times from a variety of different perspectives. Biblical passages put it this way: *"The kingdom of God is within you."*

Thus, in a manner of speaking, the ability to perceive God is a direct consequence of our biology. The neuronal connections of the human mind become the instrument by which the Creator is conceived and perceived. No other living organism or technological innovation possesses the requisite discernment capabilities. The unmistakable conclusion that arises from this understanding is that we, as His human creation, are incredibly special and favored above all other living creatures.

In addition, there is another profound consequence of this concept. *If God is to be genuinely encountered in our world, He must be experienced privately in and through the minds of each individual, one at a time, and on a very personal and intimate level.*

The suggestion that a "God spot" exists within the mind of man is really not all that surprising. Scientists have known for some time that in higher animals as well as humans, many cognitive or mental functions are sequestered into distinctive parts of the brain's physical anatomy. Some scientists even suggest that religious experience is associated with a discrete location in the temporal lobe of the brain.[1,2] Sophisticated analytical imaging techniques have also found that seeing, hearing, analytical thought, and verbalization skills are each associated with specialized cells located in specific areas of the brain.

This type of analysis is astonishing—both highly discriminating and exacting. For example, cells in one particular part of the brain electrically activate in response to viewing moving hands and faces, but the movement of inanimate objects does not engage these cells. More intriguing is the fact that some nerve cells of the brain are stimulated by sights and sounds generated by other people, but not by similar self-generated stimuli. Such experiments suggest the existence of unique neurons (brain cells) that provide specialized information about the actions/interactions of others in contrast to the actions/interactions of self.[3]

Might this be a clue to elucidating the basis of self-awareness? Perhaps. But the real picture is likely to be much more involved and these insights probably just scratch the surface. Theoretically, even higher mental processing capabilities than those described here might be feasible if appropriate interactions/communications between different specialized neuronal regions were realized. The effects of these multiple and interconnected interactions of various parts of the brain, working in concert, would begin to approach a closer characterization of true human consciousness.

Based on these observations and many others, it seems that realms of awareness stretching beyond our current comprehension, perhaps even extending beyond our religious and scientific comfort zones, cannot be completely excluded. And remember, as astonishing as these things may be, the mind with its massive array of known and unknown dimensions is ultimately derived from the ordered biological code of a person's genes.

Understanding of these biological processes is improving quickly and dramatically. Scientists have discovered, dissected, and validated the secrets to many biological mysteries that were virtually inconceivable even two decades ago.

In a similar sense, the biology of the mind, which has long been an unyielding scientific frontier, may eventually yield its intimate secrets to the experimental analysis of neurobiologists. If progressive scientific trends continue, the inconceivable of today will become tomorrow's reality. Fortunately or unfortunately, depending upon one's point of view, scientific advancements like these are likely to create significant alterations in how we view ourselves, the world, and also God.

There can be no doubt that the functioning human mind involves immense complexity. Consequently, some of the ideas that

I have shared with you in this section are somewhat simplistic and forward-looking at the present time. The conscious mind is still a great unknown, and the possibility that human consciousness contains an actual physical location to perceive/sense God is still an open question. Consciousness itself appears to emanate from multiple overlapping neural centers in the brain.[4] But regardless of whether a discrete physical location is involved or whether it is a more generalized awareness arising from interacting neural networks, the message is still clear: Springing up from within, we sense that we are created for a purpose that extends beyond the fundamental logic of our basic biology.

Perhaps God has created us with discerning minds and a consciousness for a very specific and vital purpose—to perceive Him. If this is the case, then the good news is that God is *not* far away. He may even be closer than we ever imagined. When we each personally embrace this possibility, and subsequently experience the genuine fellowship of God, the connection and the conviction of His reality will remain within forever.

Embedded Files

Entering into Relationship with God

19

The previous chapter suggests that in a manner of speaking, God provides a mechanism for His creation to connect with Him by working through our minds. This evokes a reasonable and logical question: How might we unlock and utilize this connection to discern our fullest potential as human beings?

Hidden deep within the hard drive and tiny microchip arrays, a personal computer contains coded instructions for many software programs. Each program specifies precise mathematical commands directing the computer to carry out a set of specialized functions. The speed and accuracy with which these programs execute their instructions are nothing less than astounding. In addition, many separate software programs can run simultaneously, interfacing and interacting with one another in a variety of sophisticated ways as the user employs them to calculate, analyze, interpret, and predict. The mind-numbing information-processing power exhibited by modern computer systems demonstrates the spectacular potential of these human creations. Applications such as word-processing, spreadsheet analysis, sophisticated simulations, and robotic manipulations are just a few of the functions that are commonplace.

One thing I discover when using my own personal computer is my tendency to routinely use the same software programs day after day to accomplish my tasks. Even if better programs exist, I usually stick to those with which I am most familiar, and I have followed this routine on a daily basis for years. On rare occasions, when I take the initiative to open my program file folder, I discover a large variety of software program titles, most of which I do not recognize. Frankly, the function of many of them is beyond me, and my curiosity usually is not keen enough to further investigate their content. The programs located in the program folder have always been fully available to me, but I have simply never opened them to explore their possible use and value to me.

But what would happen, if after years of familiar routine, I one day came upon a particular program that had previously gone unnoticed? The program was an integral built-in feature of my computer all along, but in the daily grind of life and work I had simply failed to notice its presence and to check it out. Now, after all this time, my attention is suddenly riveted to the program's glowing green icon on the screen. I hesitate for a moment, wondering what will happen if I open the dormant program and learn the content of its hidden files. A flurry of thoughts race through my mind:

What if the program is of no use to me?

Will it be yet another time-waster, like so many others?

Will it be too hard or take too long to understand and use?

Will its analytical processing capability provide valid information that can be fully trusted?

What if it contains virus components that could interfere with other essential programs within my computer?

Will its requirements for use make my life harder?

And why is yet another program needed? Life is already complicated and confusing enough. Let's just keep things simple! And after all, is it not true that only feeble-minded people need assistance from an outside source to cope with their problems or improve their lives? Certainly I do not want to be perceived as weak and needing any sort of crutch.

Fear, insecurity, even arrogance and an inordinate and unhealthy sense of independence all weigh in, perhaps even convincing me that the liabilities of opening the program far outweigh any reasonable benefit. After all, I may be perfectly pleased with my life just as it is.

In the final analysis, the inability to make a decision freezes me into a permanent state of inaction. And unfortunately—as is often the case at times like these—inaction is, in fact, an action. The program remains closed.

But on the other hand, if I am receptive to the new opportunity on a personal level and not immobilized by the fear of failure or of what I might find, then perhaps the program is indeed worth a try. The files of information and instructions within could even make my life much better, propelling me to levels of understanding and comprehension I had never before imagined. Maybe it would even open the door to a wonderful new world of life, happiness, and fulfillment.

As I stare at the blinking icon before me, I know a decision must be made. I can take a chance and click "open," or simply turn away and continue to experience life at the ordinary level to which I am accustomed. It is a pivotal decision. Nothing happens on its own. As long as the program is unopened, it will remain dormant forever—its potential never explored or experienced.

Opening the Files

It seems to me that a similar biologically coded program of sorts exists within each of us. This program's function is very clear: It is designed to lead us to God. Will we open it and give Him a chance?

In a way, the program is a brand new proposition. It fosters a view of life that places relatively little value on the physical components of our existence. Instead, it purposely looks past the physical elements and focuses upon a search for higher spiritual purpose. It may even require a reorientation of our current ways of thinking. But when we open the program and change our primary focus, we gradually acquire a new perspective concerning the things that matter most to God.

On the surface, adopting this approach to life seems extremely easy: It simply requires the acknowledgment that a "God program" might exist. But in reality, a greater commitment is necessary.

Every day the physical world screams for our attention, attempting to tell us who we are, what we should value, and where we should be going. In short, it tries to sell us on principles and priorities that have little ultimate significance to the Random Designer.

Therefore, if progress is to be made, more resolute action is needed. Adjusting our thinking to God's program requires that we quiet our minds and focus our attention and consciousness away from all of the misguided "noise."

To open the God files requires a consistent, intentional effort and a conscious choice to courageously and resolutely put aside things that interfere with our attempts to find the peace that God offers to us.

While opening the files is a bit more challenging than simply clicking a blinking icon on a computer terminal, I have come to believe that it is not hard. There are many ways to open the files and communicate with God. *Religious form is not nearly as significant as one's mindset and attitude.* For many people, opening the files may be as simple as speaking aloud to God. One might call it meditation, prayer, talking, communication—whatever you like. However, regardless of the terms used, it is my experience that when I regularly approach God with a genuine and sincere desire to touch Him, and with no other agenda than to be in His presence, He opens my mind and reveals Himself to me. Prayer is really not hard. It is actually quite easy. It is simply talking and listening to God.

One clear evidence of the value of prayer is that in ways that I do not yet fully understand, as time goes on, we are drawn to it and also to Him. When life is good, we think of Him. When life is bad, we think of Him. We begin to think of Him in all situations. And as we are drawn to His presence, we slowly but surely develop a subtle, but continuously growing appetite for the mind of God.

Motives Matter to God

So it appears the Random Designer has paved a path to Himself via our biological makeup. It takes the form of a strong, instinctive and built-in desire that draws us continually toward Him. The result is a mind-mediated communication channel allowing us to directly connect and cultivate our relationship with Him.

However, simply possessing the desire or being aware of the potential for communication is not enough: It is possible to enter relationships for the wrong reasons—both relationships with others and also relationship with God. And, as everyone knows, the effects of improper attitudes or motives can be devastatingly counterproductive.

Think about it. How do we respond to someone whose primary motivation for relationship is selfish, personal gain?

Quite possibly there may not be a stronger negative human emotion than the feelings of anger and betrayal we experience at being manipulated by someone. This is especially the case if we discover that the manipulation is based upon feigned sincerity. Everyone has experienced these feelings at some point in time. In fact, the closer the perceived quality of the relationship, the more hurtful the consequences become. Even minor deceptions from loved ones can be discouraging.

Some years ago, my office telephone rang late in the afternoon. I picked up the phone and immediately recognized the voice of our youngest son Phillip.

"Hi, Dad. How are you?"

"I'm fine, Phillip," I replied.

"How's work going?"

"It's going quite well, Phil. Thanks for asking"

"So are you having a good day?" he continued.

"Well, yes, Phil. Why are you being so kind and considerate of me today?"

"Oh, I just wanted to see how you were doing," he said.

By this point in the conversation, I was becoming suspicious. From the tone of Phillip's voice, I could tell that this was not a simple courtesy call to find out how dear old dad was doing. His unusual interest and concern for me were more than a bit suspect. In fact, they were dead giveaways. Phillip wanted something, and I was being manipulated to help him fulfill his desire. I decided to come right to the point.

"So why did you call me, Phil?" I asked, trying to maintain an even and inquisitive tone.

"Oh, I thought I would just call and say hello," he replied, continuing in the same vein.

Although his voice still sounded clear and innocent, by this time I think even Phillip was beginning to realize I was on to him.

"Okay, Phil, I am your father. I know you better than anyone and I can tell you want something. So what is it? Do you want Kyle or Graham to spend the night, or is it something else?"

Well, you can guess the rest of the story. Indeed, the call was really about inviting his friend Graham to spend the night.

Funny, isn't it? A loving and connected father could not fail to find humor in a nine-year-old's lack of sophistication during such an interaction. In fact, I still smile inside when I recall this exchange. However, the sadder part of the story is that my son, like every human being before and after him, will soon enough learn to be much more convincing in his deception.

Interpersonal exchanges involving more significant issues, which seem to be based upon loving and sincere desires for relationship and connection, suddenly become repugnant when we realize that we are being manipulated for selfish gain. Such experiences are so repulsive that we can hardly tear ourselves away and break fellowship fast enough. And once a person's trust and faith have been betrayed, every part of that relationship, at least for a time, is shaken to the core.

So what can we take from this discussion?

It seems to me that one of the primary desires of the Random Designer is to bring His human creation to Himself. And He calls to each of us from within the deepest recesses of our minds. But just as with human interpersonal interactions, our motives really do matter. If we approach Him with an agenda, enter His presence to impress Him or others, seek His favor for personal gain, or for any other selfish reason, the connection will simply fail. In the same way that a father is put off by attempted manipulation by his son, so God does not savor being manipulated or used.

Perhaps the most disappointing aspect of this selfish behavior to God is that it is a superhighway leading right back to the most primitive elements of our existence—a direct throwback to the limited random design paradigm of self-interest and basic physical survival. He will not have any part of our plans or reveal His mind to us when we approach Him in this way. He has called us to a much higher standard and His expectations are consistent.

How can we know these things are genuinely true? There is only one way. It is in the reality of personal experience. Pastors can preach it. Churches and schools can teach it. But until we independently take the first step, we will never fully understand. It requires initial faith and hope, but taking the first step is not difficult. In fact, it is really not an obstacle at all, but rather a wonderful opportunity.

So go ahead. Open the files. When we muster the courage to genuinely seek Him, then, and only then, He will softly speak to us. He will even welcome us. As a result, for the first time in our lives, we gradually begin to experience an inner peace that comes from entering into the covenant relationship for which we were created. The greatest joys and the most wonderful contentment await our decision.

A Choice and a Chance

A Decision of Opportunity and Destiny

20

Something magical and even sacred seems to surround the creation of a brand new human being. On a sub-cellular level, a microscopic tango is initiated within the nucleus of living cells, where replicating chromosomes, which provide the instructions for making living cells and determining a person's unique individual characteristics, reside. As sperm cells in males and egg cells in females are formed, these information-packed chromosomes vibrate, jostle, and slip over one another in an apparent disorganized heap within the nuclear confines of the reproductive cells. Following this delicate, but deliberate dance, the chromosomes then randomly segregate from one another, miraculously finding their way into the newly formed sperm or egg cell.

Later, at the instant of conception when a sperm and egg productively collide, a completely new and absolutely unique human genetic identity possessing unimaginable potential comes into existence. In fact, using the term unique to describe this new living being is a huge understatement. Other than identical twins (and even these individuals are not truly identical), no one else on the planet is put together in precisely the same way as you or me—never has been and never will be. The mathematical odds against such a genetic event are simply too great.

Thus, from the time of our birth, each individual embarks upon a special and distinct developmental track. At first the biological survival instincts reign supreme, leading to a single-minded effort to obtain the warmth and nourishment necessary for physical survival. But as time passes and the mental capacities mature, an awareness of a latent spiritual dimension to our being gradually develops as well. Inevitably a point is reached when this spiritual inkling and perception of God's existence can no longer be disregarded, and each of us is called upon to make a decision. Our response is pivotal. Whole worldviews and value systems hinge upon it, and passions, priorities, and life pursuits will all be influenced accordingly. For realistically, without a personal belief and conviction that our lives hold higher purposes and meanings than mere physical survival and the accumulation of material things, life has little of lasting value to offer.

Therefore, even though each of us is biologically unique, a common, yet critical decision is uniformly prescribed for all, regardless of class, race, social status, or position. It is posed to us as a simple, but direct question: *Will we believe?*

It seems a remarkably simple proposition, requiring very little additional explanation. But the question itself raises several others. For instance, why would a loving Creator spend billions of years to create mankind and then promptly insert such a rigid and definitive precondition to relationship? What purpose does such a requirement serve? And why does choice seem to be such a crucial element of His design?

The answers to these questions may literally encompass a complete worldview and philosophy, perhaps even filling the pages of a thick theological treatise. Or, on the other hand, perhaps the answers are much simpler.

It appears to me that God is acutely aware of a truth relating to our world and its human inhabitants that we often forget. And although it may sound trite, I believe it gets right to the heart of the matter.

Intimate and fulfilling relationship can never be required. It can only be offered and then accepted. Without the possibility of rejection, there is no genuine opportunity for meaningful connection.

Think of it. Can I command my wife to genuinely love me? Can I require my sons to truly love, respect, and want to be with me? Can I dictate that my friends, acquaintances, employees, business associates, or even my extended family like me? Of course not!

But knowing the futility of coercion does not seem to hinder us from trying. Our innate, built-in biological needs for love and relationship are strong and all encompassing. When these needs for close intimate relationship are not met in the proper manner, we are often tempted to use others for self-gratification or allow various shallow substitutes to enter and fill our lives in their stead.

> An intimate, meaningful, and fulfilling relationship cannot be required. It can only be offered! Without the possibility of rejection, there is no opportunity for meaningful connection.

Deep inside, I believe that each of us wants to be part of something greater than ourselves. We long to be members of a winning team or associate with a person or group of people who will value us as unique individuals. To partially fulfill this need, we might link ourselves with winning sports teams, a preferred political party, a special individual, or an elite organization. But the fickleness of this approach is evident for all to see. Observe what happens to most sports fans' support and allegiance when their favorite team suddenly slumps into an extended losing streak. Unless one is a member of that strange and enigmatic group known as Chicago Cub fans (maybe next year!), the loyalty quickly dissipates and the search begins in earnest for a new winner with which to associate. Perhaps the most telling reflection of this human need for belonging is seen in the enormous lengths we will pursue to gain the approval and admiration of others.

As fragile beings, we face a quandary. And while we routinely try to skirt or deny the truth, sooner or later we must meet the issue head on. We can never force someone else to love us. In the final analysis, unless the response to an offer of relationship is freely reciprocated, the relationship can never be experienced at the highest levels.

This take-it or leave-it proposition may be difficult to live out, especially for those who possess a strong desire and inner compulsion to control their world and the people who live within their particular sphere of influence. In a way, it appears to be another paradox—an overwhelming liability and an awesome opportunity all wrapped into one. The only way to experience a truly loving and satisfying relationship with another is to unreservedly grant them their freedom—*to completely relinquish control.*

When we release others to choose for themselves, we offer one of the greatest gifts that can be given. And this singular act of relinquishing our perceived control over another creates the potential for a most wonderful, but unexpected result. Powerful energy is released, and transforming relational forces begin to materialize between the participants. Sounds like something everyone would desire. However, there is also a significant danger to the proposition—a very real potential negative consequence that can result from ceding our personal right to control others. It is the clear and unmistakable risk of rejection, and with this rejection comes a whole potpourri of potentially powerful and painful emotional consequences: We can be deeply hurt.

So it appears that there is a risk involved. In order to experience the most meaningful relationship with another, we must be willing to become vulnerable—mustering the courage to take a chance on a relationship.

The eternal significance of this principle is crystal clear: God apparently has a similar plan for His relationship with us. In a very real sense, He has made Himself vulnerable to rejection by His own creation. In fact, God seems to value genuine, voluntary, and loving relationship so much that He relinquishes to us the absolute and sole right to determine our own destiny. We can choose to believe in Him or, at the opposite extreme, to categorically deny Him. Indeed, in the Biblical account of creation, at the very moment the Creator brought His human creation into existence, one of His first recorded actions was to promptly grant them the right to act against His will. But the beauty in this plan is that by doing so, He affirms and values us at the highest possible level.

Consequently, it appears that one of the central features of the Random Designer's master plan at all levels of existence is a built-in freedom to stumble and fail. He understands that for real, genuine, and meaningful relationship to be found, our love for each other *and* our love for Him must be a free and willing response. Nothing else will ever suffice. And this realization and understanding present us with a most wonderful and potentially life-altering opportunity; to answer the question with a resounding "yes!"

With an affirmative response, for the first time, we are able to take charge of our own lives. We can begin to understand why humanity possesses so many shared values, principles, and priorities. We also begin to appreciate how selfishness and its associated behaviors produce such powerful negative consequences for relationship and for mankind in general. Most importantly, the innate senses and values that are a part of our biological being can finally function as they were intended—as a guide to lead us more efficiently toward Him. We can actually begin to live fulfilled and satisfying lives—lives that are consistent with God-given principles and shared moral persuasions. We can begin to reflect His true nature.

Can we reject the existence of God and the relationship He offers? Of course!

But in this world where logical consequences arise from every action or inaction, a decision to reject Him leads to direct and decisive outcomes: There will be no genuine peace of mind, no hope in the midst of our physical suffering, and little prospect of discovering ultimate meaning or purpose in life.

For better or worse, science cannot provide significant insights or solutions in this arena. Only a personal decision and vital experience can lead to a true understanding. I, for one, do not want to live a life that proclaims or even implies there is no God and no universal good. Probably no one does! *We may be created from the forces of chaos, but that does not mean life is without purpose.*

The content of this chapter leads to one simple question: Is the opportunity to discover genuine relationships with each other and also with the Creator and to be active participants in His unfolding plan for our world, worth the risk of rejection?

The Random Designer must think so, for apparently He designed it this way. But the question is a serious one, with extremely high stakes and serious ramifications. It requires a choice and a chance. To refuse His offer is to automatically forego relationship with Him. And if God is real, what greater tragedy is there than to miss such a grand opportunity and adventure? One might even suggest that He has created each of us precisely for this moment of decision. Nevertheless, He cannot, or will not, violate His laws. He understands that true love and relationship cannot be coerced. He simply invites each of us to quiet our minds and enter in.

God's Will

*A Confusing Concept
Becomes Crystal Clear*

21

There is much talk in religious and everyday circles today about understanding God and knowing His will. But what *is* God's will for our lives? Is everything planned in advance or do we discover it in an ongoing dynamic process? And to what extent can we hope for or expect God to reveal His will to us as individuals?

As a university professor, questions regarding God's will routinely surface, particularly among students who are contemplating lifelong career options. While most people have probably considered this idea at some time or another, the question is not restricted to career choices. It also encompasses a much larger dimension, playing itself out in our everyday lives as we live and work with one another.

I understand that many of our thoughts regarding God's will are direct by-products of our religious upbringing and overall concepts of God, including how He relates to us and how we should relate to Him. Consequently, it is no surprise that people hold widely divergent views regarding the nature of God's will and how it might be best understood. For this reason, I strongly believe tolerance should prevail.

People often ask, "Does God have a plan and a design for my life?" Sometimes it is phrased even more succinctly: "Does God have a specific vocation in mind for me? A specific spouse? A specific lifestyle? A specific type of home in a specific geographical location?"

In short, this approach implies there exists a detailed blueprint to which each of us must adhere if we are to be called faithful. Others suggest God is more aloof—creating the world and then maintaining a relative "hands-off" role in His creation's subsequent development.

Frankly, it is sometimes difficult to know how to think and feel about such ideas. There are so many variables and facets to life, and each deserves consideration as a part of the overall equation. Consequently, it seems to me that neither of these two explanations offers a complete nor sufficient answer.

To be sure, many people strongly believe in some variation of the blueprint approach. According to this way of thinking, God's will in every detail has been established in advance, and every insignificant experience is preordained for a specific purpose. It is then up to each individual to work hard and strive to discover the details of this established plan.

While such a belief system may work fine for some people, most of us would find it difficult to believe that life truly operates in this manner: It is simply too rigid. Practical experience suggests that there is far too much variability in the world for this concept to fit neatly into an ordered package. Likewise, a totally aloof, uncaring God is even more unattractive. So if these approaches are untenable, a suitable, more realistic alternative must be sought.

One possibility is that God provides universal principles for us to follow when making daily decisions, and then leaves the fine details up to us. If we effectively discern these principles and act on them appropriately, He smiles with pleasure as we live out those priorities in our relationship with Him, our relationships with others, and in other aspects of daily living. For me, this approach presents a more flexible and plausible framework for faith mostly because it acknowledges the world as it truly reveals itself.

As a father, I see many parallels between my personal relationship with God and the relationship between a father and his son. Consider the intense emotions a loving father feels toward his son. Is it possible that these characteristics are mirrored in the sentiments God holds toward His human creation? Knowing how much I care for my sons, I find this thought both appealing and comforting.

When our oldest son, Jeremiah, completed his undergraduate college degree, he left us for a new life in a distant state. Along with his beautiful bride, he is now beginning his adult life on his own. There are many choices for him to make—some of them vocational, but not all. In this new setting where he desires and also deserves his independence, I often wonder what my role as his father should be.

Should I be an active participant? A passive observer? An encourager and supporter? And to what extent?

With so much to consider, it might seem nearly impossible to get it right, but I am thinking it really is not difficult at all. You see, in a manner of thinking, I am really not too concerned with the direction Jeremiah decides to follow for his vocational career. I am more than happy to let him decide this matter completely for himself. I am also content to trust his judgment concerning interactions and relationships with others. Along the way, there will be days of great pleasure and also days of pain. And although I would like to shield him from the pain, I cannot. If he is to become mature, he must be free to experience everything associated with the paths he chooses. After all, it is his life, and in the final analysis, he can only fashion it properly if he is the one who does it.

I will readily confess, however, that in another way I am deeply concerned about my son and daughter-in-law, the choices they make, and the life that they build together. My son and I have a strong relationship. I love and care for him deeply. And although I may not always demonstrate this love as well as I would like, I believe that he is aware of my concern and watchful eye. We both know his success is my success, his pain is my pain, and I share in his joys and also in his sorrows.

Do you catch a glimpse of what I am saying?

My son can be a software engineer, a farmer, a business executive, a teacher, a plumber, a custodian, even a politician, and I will still love him. My will for him is not really very concerned with his career choice. I have deeper desires for him that far surpass these everyday decisions.

However, as his father, one thing *is* extremely important to me. In fact, it matters more than anything else. For more than two decades, I invested virtually everything I had and owned into the life of this special and unique individual. And now that I have freely released him to become his own person, my deepest desire is that he return to me, affirming my most cherished values and seeking to maintain a close relationship. For me, fatherhood offers no greater satisfaction or reward.

Of course, in a manner of speaking the father/son bond will always be strong. However, the strength of this second-connect is different, extending beyond any relationship we had in the past. When my son returns to me of his own volition, he becomes much more to me than he was before. He now becomes my close and personal friend.

Who knows? With time, my son may even begin to develop similar life perspectives as his father. But the most important thing I wish for him is that he comes to understand that no matter what happens to him in the physical dimension, which I cannot control, his father loves him in ways he had previously never known or imagined possible.

How does it make me feel when my children return to me? Frankly, there is nothing else in this world that rivals the feeling—cycle complete, mission accomplished! I suspect all loving and caring parents feel the same.

And although there are huge differences in scale, I cannot help but think that a similar story plays out between us and God. For in a very real sense, one of God's primary purposes appears to be that we simply return to Him, of our own free will, to establish an intimate and genuine relationship. And just as a son learns the perspectives and values of his father over the course of a lifetime, so we too, if we desire, can acquire an increasingly clearer understanding and perception of the nature of God.

So what is the translation? Does God really have a plan and purpose for our lives? You bet He does! But it is vastly different than many have thought. Instead of a complicated, preordained, connect-the-dots blueprint that we must hopelessly struggle to decipher throughout our lifetime, it is based upon universal moral and spiritual principles and shared human values which are not all that difficult to know and understand.

God's will is simple. Virtually anyone can figure it out!

It is a call to come home—to make an effort to connect with the Creator and live in close, vital relationship with Him.

The Rewards of Perseverance

Growing in Our Relationship with God

22

"*Every journey begins with the first step*." Like me, I am sure you have probably heard these words many times. They speak to the importance of starting—of beginning a new task and moving forward from that point. Perhaps it is running a marathon, starting a new job, embarking upon a rigorous course of study, or establishing a relationship. But another important aspect of our lives seems to receive much less emphasis—finishing; mustering the courage and resolve to persevere, and complete what is started.

In the arena of relationships, finishing well is even more vital. The greatest rewards are reserved for those who stay the course and nurture their relationships over the long haul.

In many ways, our culture is not conducive to long-term commitments. In a world driven by competition, where instant gratification, self-interest, and success defined in terms of winning generally rule the day, long-term commitments are often neglected. Sadly, our minds become preoccupied by self-indulgent passions. Emotionally and spiritually paralyzed, our perspective becomes blinded, and we ourselves become the ultimate victims.

The truth is, relationships are so delicate and fragile that even a single word or deed can easily be destructive. A sign posted in the cafeteria of our local middle school catches the idea well. It reads as follows: "*Friendship is earned by many, many, many, many kindnesses. Unfortunately, it can be lost by only one unkindness.*"

When I visit the school and see these words, I am reminded that cultivating a strong ongoing relationship is a give-and-take proposition, requiring intentional effort from *each participant*. The best bonds of relationship do not develop overnight, and even the most rewarding connections in life never fully "arrive." They are a creation in progress.

I have always found it interesting that at the point of imminent death, virtually everyone 'gets religion.' They suddenly realize that religious faith and the interpersonal relationships in their lives are what matter most. In light of this understanding, the content of this chapter is a strong plea for patience and perseverance. I am convinced that wonderful relationships and even heavenly rewards await you and me—indeed everyone who patiently and passionately presses on.

An Unexpected Surprise

It was the first day of my second year in college. One of my friends caught my attention from across the student center, calling me over to introduce her new roommate. The roommate was a slender, pretty brunette with an easygoing demeanor and fun-loving smile. Her name was Sally. To my discredit, being a busy and preoccupied science major, I must confess that I took little notice of her during those early days of the term.

However, in the following weeks, I did notice something unusual. As a French and Spanish teaching major, Sally's classes met in different academic buildings than mine. However, I still bumped into her on occasion at various locations around campus. At the time, I thought these meetings were coincidental. I later learned they were not random encounters at all. Our first date was the annual university Christmas party, and a year and a half later we were married.

Those first days of married life were simply the best! Like many young couples, we thought life would never be better. Our relationship flourished over time as we patiently and deliberately labored together to manage the many challenges associated with school, work, and raising a family.

One day, about thirteen years into our marriage, I vividly recall an unexpected and unusual event. I was standing on the front porch of our new country home, alone with my thoughts, when suddenly I felt that something very dramatic had changed. The experience was so overwhelming that it immediately captured my full attention. For some reason, at that particular moment, I sensed that Sally had become much more to me than just my spouse. Somewhere along the way, emerging from times of happiness, sadness, laughter, pain, the unexpected, and the routine, she had become my dearest and closest friend. In a moment I will never forget, I suddenly realized I could not imagine living my life without her.

In retrospect, I can see the unfolding of the events that led up to this new awareness. They had been gradual, even imperceptible while they were occurring, but suddenly everything crystallized in a single sparkling epiphany. It was an unexpected and deeply personal awakening. On this life-changing day, I acquired a more complete perspective and understanding of how the best relationships in life work.

Since then, the years have definitely been full. We have laughed, cried, worked, and played side by side. We have also experienced a full array of challenges, disappointments, and joys related to the raising of our four sons. And like everyone else, we have endured the heart-ripping pain that accompanies the deaths of close family members and friends. In short, life has been very real.

Now, after all these years and varied experiences, we recognize that our marriage still deserves our best efforts. We watch in wonder and awe as our children establish new relationships and begin the cycle of life all over again. The time has been so short, it sometimes seems like a dream. But it has not been a dream. It has been a wonderful and full life. Today, as we continue to live and love together, I have a suspicion that Sally and I are just beginning to achieve a perspective that allows us to see life as it really is. For me, the message of that day on the front porch was clear: *If we are faithful to our commitments, there are occasional unexpected "aha" moments on the horizon. Things present, but previously unseen, suddenly focus into a sharply define image.*

Looking back to our wedding day, I smile at how naive I was at the time. I could never have fathomed such a wonderful gift would one day be mine. I am also convinced that our relationship would never have grown to this point without a diligent and conscientious effort from *both of us* to remain committed for the long haul. Tempered and seasoned over many years, we have become closer than we ever could have imagined.

In a marvelous and mystical way, I am discovering that this is how relationships are meant to be—even our relationship with God. Remember, true relationships and meaningful connection cannot be defined or coerced. They can only be experienced. So, for those of us fortunate enough to find a true soul-mate, we are granted the opportunity to experience one of God's greatest gifts to His creation.

I am also discovering that in our relationship with God, as with other people, a deeper conviction and awareness of His presence often sneaks up on us—wonderfully bursting upon our consciousness when we least expect it. This new awareness may be nurtured by a friend, a parent, a church, a teacher, a specific life experience, or by an intensely personal revelation of His love and care.

The promise for all is that when we are consistently committed to seeking God in prayer and meditation, as well as in lifestyle, He gradually begins to make Himself known. Our minds become attuned to His mind, and over time, we incrementally change, developing new perspectives of how life should work. Ultimately, as part of this process, we are offered the most precious gift of all, His gift of peace.

There is no apparent clue as to when or where this magical moment of revelation will occur. It cannot be scheduled in advance, manufactured, or required. We can only watch patiently in faith, believing the day will eventually arrive if we diligently seek Him.

So will we keep looking? There is really nothing to fear. Just as a loving father watches over the children he created, so the Random Designer continuously calls from the deepest recesses of our minds. All He asks of us is an honest, patient, and persevering faith. My sincere hope is that one day, just as occurred in my relationship with Sally, and also with Him, you too will experience a deepening sense of His presence, that He is more real than physical life itself, and that you cannot imagine living the rest of your life without Him.

Higher Order Random Design

Innate God-Given Value is for Everyone!

23

Throughout this book, I have made the case that within the constraints imposed by mutation and natural selection, simple forms of life sequentially build upon one another to construct continuously more advanced biological beings. The primary goal of this process appears to be that of survival, whether it is survival of the biological molecules themselves, or the preservation of living creatures that result from the interaction of these molecules. Thus, at the biochemical, cellular, and organism levels of biology, the basic random design rule of "self first" uniformly receives the highest priority.

However, in this chapter, we will see that in a most remarkable way, the "self first" concept also serves in another capacity, functioning as a conduit, which propels biology well beyond its primary directive of survival.

In very subtle, yet enormously significant ways, the random design paradigm can actually become self assembling and self-propagating. Biological systems that function in this way are particularly noteworthy because their constituents begin to display rudimentary elements of higher level behavior—traits like commitment, sacrifice, and benevolence. I call these systems "higher order random design."

To define this concept and explore its role in living things, I will start with a succinct functional definition: Higher order random design occurs when random processes are no longer completely random. Stated another way, higher order random design occurs when randomized processes no longer execute their random roles in complete isolation. Instead, they become significant components of a systematized and coordinated organizational design scheme.

I realize that these definitions may seem somewhat confusing, but higher-level processes are like that. But if we are only willing to acknowledge and accept easy explanations for complex biological phenomena, life's most profound secrets may never be revealed. The truth is that complicated and integrated design structures rarely give up their secrets easily, and comprehending difficult concepts requires diligent and thorough study. In addition, the concept of higher order random design is an idea steeped in irony. For as strange as it may seem, now, within the broader parameters of biology, *organized and deliberate randomness actually becomes a primary goal.*

Does biology really develop organized assemblies charged with the task of promoting randomness? And even if these systems actually do exist, what possible good might arise from them? Statements such as "deliberate disorder" or "structured randomness," while describing higher order random design quite well, also seem to be inherently counterintuitive: Structure and randomness do not seem to go together.

Nevertheless, in spite of our preconceptions, traditions, and perspectives on the matter, the Random Designer evidently sees the situation much differently.

Designed Randomness

In a modern biological context, it is hard to argue with the reality of empirical observation. From the lowest to the highest levels of life, the world of biology is dynamic, never ceasing to surprise us. And the story it tells is an intriguing one. Whenever biological systems or living organisms face challenging problems, they are remarkably adept at finding imaginative solutions to these challenges, using the previously discussed mechanisms of basic random design. The solutions to biological problems are then promptly integrated into the continuously evolving and developing fabric of life.

The inescapable conclusion is that random design principles have immense value to life. Consequently, it should come as no surprise to discover that biology has established elaborate and deliberate mechanisms to create, maintain, and even extend random processes within many of the highest life forms. Indeed, human beings and many other advanced life forms already possess such designed randomness strategies as essential elements of their beings. To provide some insight into this idea, I will describe one such biological system, and then discuss some of the possible ramifications.

The Immune System: B Cells and Antibodies

One of the most compelling examples illustrating higher order random design in biology lies within the human immune system. The immune system acts as a protective shield against the continuous onslaught of potentially harmful invaders—germs that can cause disease. Fortunately, although the immune system is an extraordinarily complex network of interacting cells, the most central features are not difficult to comprehend. Just three specialized white blood cell types carry out its most essential activities. Figure 23.1 identifies these cells and their biological roles.

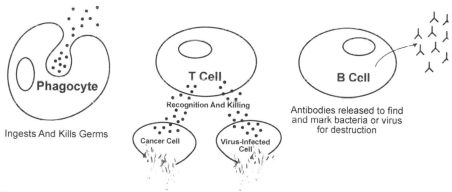

Figure 23.1   Cells of Immune System

Phagocytes are the first of these cells. They minimize disease by promptly engulfing and destroying dangerous germs that manage to enter our bodies. The second group of cells, called T cells, carries out a wide variety of supporting roles for the immune system.

The most critical assignment of these cells is to mark and kill any other cells of the body that have become cancerous or compromised by a virus infection. B cells are the third cell type of white blood cell. These cells are especially interesting because they produce the group of protective proteins we call antibodies.

During the course of a lifetime, billions of B cells are continually regenerated within each of us—millions each day. Under normal circumstances, whenever a harmful bacteria, virus, or other disease-causing agent enters the body, the appropriate B cells are activated to grow and divide. Within a couple of days, an expanded population of these B cells releases specific antibody proteins into the blood and tissues of the body. These circulating antibodies, serving as sentries, patrol the body's tissues to search for any remaining intruders. When the antibodies encounter an invader, they firmly latch onto it. This binding serves to "mark" the intruder and target it for destruction. In this manner, B cells, combined with their corresponding antibodies, play pivotal roles in maintaining a healthy state.

The critical need we have for these B cells and their protective antibody proteins is easily observed. For example, consider a rare genetic condition called Bruton's agammaglobulinemia. Individuals inheriting this condition are unable to form fully functional B cells. As a result, blood antibody levels are virtually nonexistent, thus making these people susceptible to a wide variety of infections. Only continuous medical surveillance assures their health and well-being.

Examination of the specific nature of the antibody-targeting phenomenon reveals a fascinating feature. Antibody molecules are not simply one large, amorphous single-function group. Just as human beings are similar in many respects, but individually unique, antibodies likewise share many common characteristics, but are also individually distinct. This uniqueness is most clearly seen in their specific targeting actions. An antibody molecule that recognizes and targets the influenza virus will protect us from influenza. However, this same antibody is utterly useless against the measles virus. Similarly, antibodies produced in response to *Streptococcus pneumoniae*, one of the bacteria responsible for pneumonia, will only protect against this disease—nothing else. Thus, the precision of the antibody-targeting phenomenon is exquisitely exacting. Figure 23.2 shows an example of B cells at work.

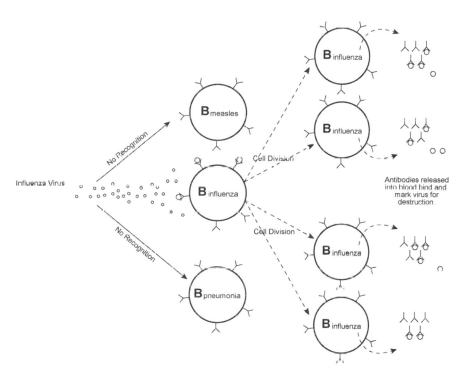

Figure 23.2   B Cells and Immunity

This strategy is remarkable in itself, but an even more astounding story takes place *within* the B cells. It turns out that during its formation, each and every B cell is genetically preprogrammed to make copies of *just one specific targeting antibody*. This is significant because scientists know that we theoretically encounter millions of potential invaders during a lifetime. With such a large number of potential attackers, each needing a specific B cell's antibody for protection, a difficult and fundamental issue arises: How can the immune system possibly make millions of different B cells along with their corresponding antibodies, and thus provide a complete system of protection? As unbelievable as it seems, biology has developed an effective remedy to deal with this life-or-death challenge.

Rather than delaying action until a problem germ comes on the scene, the immune system is proactive. It simply makes every different type of B cell that might ever be conceivably needed—*in advance!* As a result, millions of pre-made and fundamentally distinct B cells are already circulating within each of us. Therefore, regardless of what disease-causing agents nature throws at us during our lifetime, the body's defenses are already fully prepared for any and all threats. Scientists have even identified precisely how this process comes about. In short, it is a type of higher order random design.

As a B cell matures, the cell's DNA is instructed to undergo an orchestrated and highly organized series of randomized gene rearrangements. The net effect of this precisely controlled, yet randomized process is that a nearly infinite array of B cells and antibody specificities are generated from a very small number of immunity genes. *Each of the resulting B cells thus exists for a unique and special purpose. Absolutely no other B cell can fulfill its protective role in exactly the same way.* And since no one knows in advance which particular infectious agents will be encountered during a lifetime, each distinctive B cell, whether it is ever used or not, serves a critical sentry role.

The genius of such a system is inescapable. Can you glimpse the imagery? Floating within us are billions of preformed B cells, each acting individually, yet also corporately. In this way, they appear to accomplish the impossible—protecting us from virtually *anything* that might come our way. Illness will generally arise only if some component of the immune system is compromised or if the invading organism evolves a new disease-causing feature that gives it a temporary advantage. A random design system of this nature thus provides the most effective mechanism for accomplishing the goal of lifelong protection with the highest degree of certainty.

The B cell story is a lucid biological example of higher order random design. Complex biological systems and multiple independent random processes interact simultaneously to create entities that function cooperatively and productively in ways that stretch our intellect and current ways of thinking.

Remember, these biological systems are not hypothetical or theoretical. They are real! They exist as a design within a design, within yet another design.

This discussion is not meant to suggest the concept of higher order random design in any way negates or detracts from the basic random design model considered throughout this book. Indeed, individual randomness-driven elements will, of necessity, always be with us. But in this innovative and more extensive context, random processes have, in essence, been captured and harnessed to participate in a greater design system, delivering more profound and desirable effects than previously observed or even conceived.

Higher order random design is a wonderfully unifying concept and provides another striking example of how the Random Designer accomplishes His purposes through extremely unlikely avenues.

Is God truly a Random Designer? I believe overwhelming evidence tells us that He is. But He goes even further. He is also a higher order Random Designer. And in this way, He accomplishes great good for Himself and for His creation.

Random Designed God-Given Value

As amazing as these complex biological systems are, it seems to me that the most significant consequences of the higher order random design concept are the real life implications for human beings. *Indeed, we may actually be the central characters in the most magnificent higher order random design system of all time.* And if this is the case, then it follows that each of us may be part of something much, much bigger than ourselves.

Previous chapters focused on the importance of acknowledging God and establishing a personal relationship with Him. For some people, these straightforward actions in and of themselves may be sufficient and satisfying. But at some time in life, nearly everyone dreams of finding significance as part of a more transcendent plan—one extending beyond our physical senses and everyday realities, allowing us to make an eternal difference in our world. In a way, higher order random design presents just such an opportunity. For within the confines of a community, positive synergies can result from actions involving cooperation, commitment, sacrifice, and selflessness.

In the immune system example, we see that randomly formed B cells are each unique and special. As such, they make life-sustaining contributions to the overall functioning of the body.

We also are random creations! Conceived by two sexually reproducing parents, which facilitates the randomization process, we are fashioned in ways that impart to us comparable degrees of uniqueness and identity. Remember, no one is exactly the same as you or me. The implications of this fact are truly stunning. Each person possesses truly distinctive talents, aptitudes, and abilities. In addition, regardless of our personal feelings of inadequacy and sometimes limited perceptions about our own abilities, higher order random design conveys the unambiguous message to each individual that they possess intrinsic God-given value. What a gift! We are all potential participants in His overall higher order plan. And as we discover the subtle details and nuances of our individual gifts, we are presented with the opportunity to experience a wonderful, exciting, and adventurous life.

Finally, one message of higher order random design supersedes all others: *No one needs to feel inadequate or anxious about where they fit. A common purpose and path has been provided for all.* While not everyone will be the greatest, that is okay. The Random Designer is not interested in comparisons. We can rest in the design of the Creator. We are His ultimate creation—His children. And as His children, our sole responsibility is to seek His mind. In doing so, we can gradually learn to discern His priorities, discover how to utilize our talents most effectively, and learn to tap into His plans.

But one word of caution seems appropriate. We must carefully examine our motives. God's peace can only be experienced when we understand and embrace the higher order concept of selfless and generous living.

I am reminded of a quote from the martyred American missionary to South America, James Elliot. His wife, Elizabeth often quoted these words. *"He is no fool, who gives what he cannot keep, to gain what he cannot lose."*[1] To this statement I will add: Of all the many material possessions we accumulate, we cannot keep any of them.

B cells are not created for themselves. They are formed for a much higher and nobler purpose. In the same way, we also are not created just for ourselves. One day, maybe even today, when we truly recognize, understand, and act on this fact, perhaps we will begin to experience the fullness life has to offer. Above all, we will begin to catch a glimpse of ourselves as our Creator sees us—individuals of utmost value, the first and last of His creation to be made in His image.

The Ultimate Creation

A Miraculous Balancing Act Hits a Wall

24

Before the current age of modern molecular biology, the study of biology was largely a descriptive science. Scientists took their notebooks in hand and went into the field or laboratory to systematically observe, describe, and classify living organisms. But the study of life is much more than a matter of simple dissection and description. The language of life today is best deciphered in terms of the biochemistry and molecular biology of cells. This biochemical approach has yielded breath-taking insights, leading to definitive descriptions of cell molecular architecture and the molecular logic that drives and sustains all life.

As described earlier, many of the most revolutionary discoveries of biology have emerged from the field of genetics. As scientists subject the genetic mechanisms of life to closer scrutiny, the story that unfolds becomes more and more provocative and also leads to an intriguing possibility. *Biologically speaking, human beings may be the last order in a long line of created organisms.*

Although somewhat oversimplified, functionally speaking it works like this: Our chromosomes are nearly full. Little room remains for extensive gene expansion and its associated biological development. Thus, one of the hidden messages emanating from the molecules of our DNA is the suggestion that in human beings, life is nearly full-grown.

In earlier chapters I discussed the role of mutation and natural selection in developing design in higher forms of life. I explained that although mutation is generally harmful, occasional positive mutations also occur. Thus, when a gene within a cell is modified, even in a random way, the corresponding protein resulting from that gene is occasionally improved.

Organisms arising from these positive changes are better adapted to successfully carry on the next generation of life. Because the ability to generate genetic diversity is such a crucial ingredient of all living things, organisms have actually developed designed mechanisms to enhance genetic mixing and mutation. This type of process is easily recognizable: It is a variation of higher order random design.

These elegant systems continuously promote genetic diversity within us, *but they must be carefully regulated.* Remember, cells must pass their genes to the next generation with a high degree of fidelity—that is, with very few mistakes. Therefore, all life exists in a tight-wire state of continuous tension that narrowly extends through time and space. Organisms must maintain the integrity of the complex and highly evolved genes that direct the incredible processes of life. However, they have an equally important stipulation to provide mechanisms that will introduce some diversity into the genetic code, thus allowing for necessary adaptation and change.

The conclusion is abundantly clear: All life on the planet, from the beginning of time to this present moment, is the product of a precarious balancing act. Within the dual constraints of a generally harmful and relatively constant mutation rate, versus the need to faithfully preserve the best products, exquisite fine-tuning over billions of years of evolution has brought forth truly spectacular combinations of precisely constructed genes that serve to support human existence.

The result is that human genes appear to be optimized to near maximum efficiency for carrying out the most critical and essential functions of the cell. And while it is certainly good to have optimized gene combinations, this high level of refinement also has its liabilities: It tends to make us somewhat fragile and vulnerable.

Consider a mathematical consequence for complex gene systems in advanced living cells. As the number of essential genes within a cell increases and the level of fine-tuning within each gene is continually enhanced to meet the precise needs of the species, the probability also rises that life will become more difficult to maintain. Simply put, the more highly refined and integrated the genome becomes, the easier it is to mess it up. It becomes increasingly susceptible to damage caused by random mutation and change. Put yet another way, if something was only marginally functional, there would still be room for improvement via random change. But after many rounds of optimization and improvement, random changes are far more likely to cause harm than good. Thus, in highly advanced beings like humans, even very slight, subtle changes can have disastrous consequences.

Overall, as the web of biological development becomes increasingly complex, a point of diminishing returns is reached where the inherent mutation rate sets an upper limit on the total number of essential functioning genes within a cell.[1,2]

Humans appear to have approximately 30,000 genes. Is this number near the limit? While no one knows for sure what the actual limit is, based upon inherent mutation rates, some scientists suggest that human beings may be approaching the theoretical maximum number of sustainable genes. Thus, even from the scientific perspective, it appears that *human beings may indeed be the Random Designer's ultimate creation. If this is the case, then it also raises the interesting possibility that we were the goal of His creation from the beginning of time.*

Think of it! Here we are poised at this special place in time wondering who we are and considering our value in this world. And now we learn that we may be the very reason for all of life's history. We have unimaginable random-designed, God-given value.

I wonder how the Creator views all this? Could it be that finally, through nearly 5 billion long and tumultuous years of gestation, He has successfully brought forth His prize and treasure? He has created us to be the most majestic miracle of all time—human beings made in His image and destined from the start to be the special ones of His creation. And now He has placed His principles and values within us. We all innately know His standards. Look around. He has provided countless signs of His presence and love to all of creation, if only we will see with our eyes, hear with our ears, and understand with our minds. Most of all, He has paved a pathway to help us discover Him and enter into a special coveted relationship.

So my final question is quite simple: What if it is really true? Maybe we really are the goal of this incredible creative endeavor that has spanned billions of years to reach fruition. If this is the case—if all of the world's biological history has taken place just to create us, would it not be the ultimate tragedy to miss Him?

A Call to Come Home

*Finding God's Peace in a
Randomness-Driven World*

25

God, the Random Designer, has created us for a purpose. All the forces and laws of nature were put in place to bring us into existence and to convey an awareness of our acute need for Him. Each individual has significance and value in God's eyes, and everyone is invited to participate in the Creator's master plan. For some, a simple affirmative response to the invitation may suffice. Others will participate in more direct and eternally significant ways. But there are no class distinctions with the Random Designer. We are all squarely in the center of the universe's divine, unfolding drama.

Everyone wants to be on the winning team—to sense we are part of something greater than ourselves. This inborn desire to belong is a powerful force in humans—a fundamental and uniform biological feature assembled from the sequences of our genetic code and built into the neuronal fabric of our consciousness. And it finds outward expression in our everyday thoughts and actions. *This universal deep-seated desire ensures that everyone, regardless of status, position, wealth, or background, will be sufficiently drawn to Him.*

Life on earth can sometimes be an extremely difficult proposition. The reality of random design is that it prescribes a physical existence that is a never-ending uphill struggle. We long to be released from selfishness and the sometimes brutal biological bonds holding us captive in this world. However, regardless of our plight in life, a glimmer of hope radiates from the innermost recesses of the soul. It is a hope that someone will show compassion and comfort us in the midst of our pain.

Deep within, I think we know the one we are searching for is God. We sense the glow is there, but we are hesitant to trust Him. We have

189

been disappointed and let down so many times before. In our most honest moments, we have sometimes wondered if He is even there at all. We want to believe. We know we *should* believe. But wariness and fear set in, flooding our minds with apprehension and doubt. So we deny the hope, hide it, or simply ignore it. And those feelings of uncertainty are understandable. For in a world that greatly values physical evidence and scientific proof, it is sometimes scary to take a step based upon faith alone. It seems like an intolerable risk to believe the inner hope is genuine when science and the senses seem so silent on the issue.

So how much evidence will suffice to persuade? Will it always be just a little more than yesterday? Will we rigidly require the performance of perceived miracles before we believe that there is a God who created us and brought us to this point of decision?

It seems to me that we are an incredibly shortsighted species. Abundant evidence for the existence of God is all around us. It whispers its wisdom in the minuscule molecular architecture of the tiniest living organisms and shouts its message from the loftiest mountaintops and faraway galaxies. Most amazingly of all, from the random forces and elements of nature He has mysteriously fashioned productive pathways and created us from clay. And now, after eons of preparation, He extends an offer to connect with Him through the vehicle of our conscious minds and to experience Him in the closeness and intimacy of a mystical, yet intensely personal relationship.

When all is said and done, the ultimate objective and purpose in life appears to boil down to this one crucial action—to answer His invitation to relationship. If this is the case, then what further evidence is required before we say "yes?" He is the hope that never goes away—unless we send Him away.

It may have taken a long time for the human race to reach this extraordinary place and time, but what is a billion years to a timeless God? The truth is that in a very real sense, we are all random travelers in this randomness-driven world. But random does not mean unimportant or without design! In fact, it may be a much greater miracle than we could possibly conceive. For embedded within the apparently random and transient vapor of our short sojourn here, there lies a cryptic path. All are called to follow. And for those who can discern it, there is the promise of purpose and peace.

The plan has been established and the pathway to relationship placed within. The Random Designer invites us to journey with Him. It is a vibrant, compelling, and contemporary plan. No one need be left out, left behind, or left alone. The adventure begins with a single step of faith!

Epilogue

Random Designer is now completed, a project that has gradually taken shape in my mind over nearly fifteen years. Occasionally, during times of discouragement and uncertainty when I was searching for direction, I sensed a special closeness, urging and guidance to complete the task. These encounters were intensely personal and have spoken to me in powerful and compelling ways. Thus, *Random Designer* has been, for me, a work of both praise and worship. In addition, I believe it conveys a relevant and contemporary message for everyone.

I cannot prove God to you scientifically—no one can. And though I firmly believe that God communicates with His human creation, I cannot explain the precise mechanisms by which this occurs. I can only relate my own personal experience. This experience and relationship convinces me God is real. It also suggests that if God can make Himself known to me, He can do the same for you. It is my sincere hope and desire that you will continue listening for His voice and never give up on that possibility!

INDEX

References

Chapter 2

1. Human Genome Project information. On-line. Available from http://www.ornl.gov/hgmis/publications.html.
2. Davison, Daniel B. "The Number of Human Genes and Proteins." *Technical Proceedings of the Second International Conference on Computational Nanoscience and Nanotechnology. April 22-25, 2000. 6-11.*
3. Pope John Paul II. Written statement to Pontifical Academy of Sciences. Rome. October 22, 1996. On-line. Available from http://www.cin.org/ip2cvolu.html.
4. General Assembly of Presbyterian Church. General Assembly Affirms "God's Gift" Curriculum. Columbus, Ohio. June 15-22, 2002.

Chapter 3

1. "Einstein Explains the Equivalency of Matter and Energy." On-line. Available from http://www.aip.org/history/einstein/voice1.htm
2. Hawking, S. W. *A Brief History of Time: From the Big Bang to Black Holes*. Toronto: Bantam Books, 1998.

Chapter 4

1. "Age of Universe Confirmed." BBC News, April 25, 2002. On-line. Available from http://news.bbc.co.uk/1/hi/sci/tech/1950403.stm
2. Brack, Andre. *The Molecular Origins of Life*. Cambridge: Cambridge University Press, 1998.
3. Sagan, C., and C. Chyba. "The Early Faint Sun Paradox: Organic Shielding of Ultraviolet Labile Greenhouse Gases." *Science* 276 (1977): 1217-1221.
4. Miller, S. L. "Which Organic Compounds Could Have Occurred on the Prebiotic Earth?" Paper presented at Cold Spring Harbor Symposia on Quantitative Biology III, 1987.
5. Eye, Iris. *The Emergence of Life on Earth—A Historical and Scientific Overview*. Rutgers University Press: New Brunswick, N.J. and London, 2000.

Chapter 5

1. Fox, S. and K. Dose. *Molecular Evolution and the Origin of Life*. New York: Marcel Dekker, 1977.
2. Ferris, J. P., A.R. Hill, Jr., R. Liu, and L. E. Orgel. "Synthesis of Long Prebiotic Oligomers on Mineral Surfaces." *Nature,* 381 (1996): 59-61.
3. Ertem, G. and J.P. Ferris. "Synthesis of RNA Oligomers on Heterogeneous Templates." *Nature.* 379 (1996): 238-240.
4. Brack, Andre. *The Molecular Origins of Life*. Cambridge: Cambridge University Press, 1998.
5. Woese, C.R. and G.E. Fox, G.E. "Phylogenetic Structure of the Prokaryotic Domain: The Primary Kingdoms." Proc. Natl. Acad. Sci., USA. 74 (1977): 5088-5090.
6. Woese, C.R. "Bacterial Evolution." *Microbiology Rev.* 51 (1987): 221-271.
7. Butt, C.J., C.R. Woese, J.C. Venter, et al. "Complete Genome Sequence of the Methanogic Archaeon Methanococcus jannaschii." *Science* 273 (1996): 1058-1073.

Chapter 10

1. Pergament, Eugene, MD. "Tumor Suppressor Genes." On-line. Available from the Genetics of Cancer Resource Center. http://www.intouchlive.com/home/frames.htm?http://www.intouchlive.com/cancergenetics/p53.htm&3.
2. Malkin, David. "Germline Mutations and Heritable Cancer." *Annual Review of Genetics* 28 (1994): 443-65.
3. Alberts, Bruce, Alexander Johnson, Julian Lewis, Martin Raff, Keith Roberts, and Peter Walter. *Molecular Biology of the Cell.* 4th ed. New York: Garland Publishing, 2002.

Chapter 11

1. Prothero, Donald R. *Bringing Fossils to Life*. WCB. Dubuque, Iowa: McGraw-Hill, 1998.
2. Cowen, Richard. *History of Life*. 3rd ed. Malden, Massachusetts: Blackwell Science, Inc., 2000.
3. McKinney, Michael, L. *Evolution of Life*. Englewood Cliffs, New Jersey: Prentice-Hall, 1993.
4. Brown, George D., Jr. *Human Evolution*. Dubuque, Iowa: William C. Brown Publishers, 1995.
5. Gibbons, Ann and Michael Balter. "In Search of the First Hominids." *Science* 295 (2002): 1214-1225.

Chapter 12

1. *The Holy Bible*. New International Version. New York: International Bible Society, 1978.

2. Cann, R. L., M. Stoneking, and A. C. Wilson. "Mitochondrial DNA and Human Evolution." *Nature* 325 (1987): 31.
3. Vigilant, L., M. Stoneking, A. C. Harpending, K. Hawkes, and A. C. Wilson. "African Populations and the Evolution of Human Mitochondrial DNA." *Science* 253 (1991): 1503.
4. Paabo, S. "The Y Chromosome and the Origin of All of Us (Men)." *Science* 268 (1995): 1141.
5. Hammer, M.F. "A Recent Common Ancestry for Human Y Chromosomes." *Nature* 378 (1995): 376-378.
6. Whitfield, L. S., J.E. Suston, and P.N. Goodfellow. "Sequence Variation of the Human Y Chromosome." *Nature* 378 (1995): 379-380.
7. Fischman, J. "Evidence Mounts for Our African Origins—and Alternatives." *Science* 271 (1996): 1364.
8. Krings, M., A. Stone, R. W. Schmitz, H. Krainitzki, M. Stoneking, and S. Paabo. "Neanderthal DNA Sequences and the Origin of Modern Humans." *Cell* 90 (1997): 19-30.
9. Edelman, Gerald and Giulio Tononi. *A Universe of Consciousness—How Matter Becomes Imagination.* Boulder, Colorado: Basic Books, 2000.

Chapter 13

1. Edelman, Gerald and Giulio Tononi. *A Universe of Consciousness—How Matter Becomes Imagination.* Boulder, Colorado: Basic Books, 2000.
2. Tononi, Giulio, Ramensh Srinivasan, D. Patrick Russell, and Gerald Edelman. "Investigating Neural Correlates of Conscious Perception by Frequency—Tagged Neuromagnetic Responses." *Proc. Natl. Acad. Sciences,* USA. 95 (1998): 3198-203.
3. Chedd-Angier Prod. Co. "Scientific American Frontiers." PBS Home Video, 2000.
4. Srinivasan, R. D., Russell Patrick, Gerald Edelman, and Giulio Tononi. "Increased Synchronization of Neuro Magnetic Responses During Conscious Perception." *J. of Neuroscience* 19 no. 13 (1999): 5435-448.

Chapter 16

1. "Internet Technology." PBS Home Video, 1995.

Chapter 18

1. Carter, Rita. *Mapping the Mind.* Berkeley, California: University of California Press, 1998.
2. Newberg Andrew, Eugene D'Aquili, and Vince Rause. *Why God Won't Go Away—Brain Science and the Biology of Belief.* New York, Toronto: Ballantine Books, 2001.
3. Frith, Chris D. and Uta Frith "Interacting Minds—A Biological Basis." *Science* 286 (1999).
4. Edelman, Gerald and Giulio Tononi *A Universe of Consciousness—How Matter Becomes Imagination.* Boulder, Colorado: Basic Books, 2000.

Chapter 23

1. Elliot, Elisabeth. *Through Gates of Splendor.* Wheaton, Illinois: Tyndale House Publishers, 1981.

Chapter 24

1. Alberts, Bruce, Alexander Johnson, Julian Lewis, Martin Raff, Keith Roberts, and Peter Walter, *Molecular Biology of the Cell,* 4th ed. New York: Garland Publishing, 2002.
2. Ohta, T. and M. Kimura. "Functional Organization of Genetic Material as a Product of Molecular Evolution." *Nature* 233 (1971): 118-119.

Selected Readings

Ausich, William I. and N. Gary Lane. *Life of the Past*, 4th ed. Prentice Hall Inc., Simon and Schuster, 1999.

Behe, Michael J., *Darwin's Black Box—The Biochemical Challenge to Evolution*. Simon and Schuster, 1996.

Berra, Tim M. *Evolution and the Myth of Creationism*. Stanford University Press, 1990.

"Building a Bridge Between The Big Bang and Biology." *Science* 274 (November 1996).

Cotton, Ian. "Dr. Persinger's God Machine." *Independent on Sunday,* July 2, 1995.

"Creationism: The Debate Is Still Evolving." *USA Weekend* (April 1997),

Darwin, Charles. *The Origin of the Species*. New York: Bantam Books, 1999.

Dawkins, Richard. *The Selfish Gene*. Oxford: Oxford University Press, 1989.

Dawkins, Richard. *The Blind Watchmaker*. New York: W. W. Norton, 1987.

Denton, Michael. *Evolution: A Theory in Crisis*, 2nd ed. Adler and Adler, 1996.

Eyring, Henry. *Reflections of a Scientist*. Salt Lake City: Deseret Book Company, 1983.

Giberson, Karl. *Worlds Apart—The Unholy War Between Religion and Science*. Kansas City: Beacon Hill Press, 1993.

Gleick, James. *Chaos—Making a New Science*. New York: Viking Penguin Publishing, 1987.

Goodenough, Ursula. *The Sacred Depths of Nature*. Oxford: Oxford University Press, 1998.

Gould, Steven J. *Rocks of Ages—Science and Religion in the Fullness of Life*. Library of Contemporary Thought. Ballantine, 1999.

"How the Brain Creates the Mind." *Scientific American*, New York (December 1999).

Johnson, Phillip. *The Wedge of Truth*. InterVarsity Press, 2001.

Johnson, Phillip E. *Reason in the Balance—The Case Against Naturalism in Science, Law, and Education*. InterVarsity Press, 1995.

Johnson, Phillip E. *Darwin on Trial*. InterVarsity Press, 1993.

Johnston, Wendy K., Peter J. Unrau, Michael S. Lawrence, Margaret E. Glassner, and David P. Bartel. "RNA—Catalyzed RNA Polymerization: Accurate and General RNA—Templated Primer Extension." *Science* 292, (2001).

"Kansas Board of Education Reinstates Teaching of Evolution." *Kansas Curriculum Standards for Science Education* (February 14, 2001).

"Kansas Board of Education Bars Teaching of Evolution." *Kansas Curriculum Standards for Science Education* (August 11, 1999).

McKee, Jeffrey K. *The Riddled Chain: Chance, Coincidence, and Chaos in Human Evolution.* Rutgers University Press, 2000.

McMenamin, Mark A. S., and Dianna L. Schulte. *The Emergence of Animals—The Cambrian Breakthrough.* New York: Columbia University Press, 1990.

Miller, Kenneth. *Finding Darwin's God.* New York: Cliff Street Books, 1999.

Nelson, Craig E. and James W. Skehan. *The Creation Controversy and the Science Classroom.* National Science Teacher's Association Press.

Newberg, Andrew, Eugene D'Aquili, and Vince Rouse. *Why God Won't Go Away.* New York: Ballantine Books, 2001.

Pennock, Robert T. *Tower of Babel—Evidence Against the New Creationism.* Cambridge: MIT Press, 1999.

"Primordial Soup Researchers Gather at Watering Hole." *Science* 277 (August 22, 1997).

Prothero, Donald R., and Robert H. Dott, Jr. *Evolution of the Earth, 7ᵗʰ ed.* McGraw Hill Higher Education, 2004.

Reports—National Center for Science Education 20, no. 4 (July/Aug 2000).

Ridley, Matthew. *Genome.* New York: Harper Collins Publishers, 1999.

Ross, Hugh. *The Fingerprint of God,* 2ⁿᵈ ed. Promise Publishing Co, 1991.

"Science and God: A Warming Trend?" *Science* 277 (August 1997).

"Scientists and Religion in America." *Scientific American* (September 1989).

"Scientists Strike Back Against Creationism." *Science* 286 (October 22, 1999).

Similarities in Eucaryotic Genes, Comparative Biochemistry and Physiology. Pergamon Press 95, no. 1 (1990).

Smith, Kendric C. "Spontaneous Mutagenesis: Experimental, Genetic and Other Factors." *Mutation Research* 277 (1992): 139-162.

Teaching about Evolution and the Nature of Science. National Academy Press, 1998.

Templeton, Sir John. *Possibilities for Over One Hundredfold More Spiritual Information.* Templeton Foundation Press, 2000.

Unto Others—The Evolution and Psychology of Unselfish Behavior. Harvard University Press, 1998.

Van Till, William. B. *The Fourth Day.* Eerdmans Publishing Co., 1986.